God Speaks on
Family

Practical Wisdom for the 21ˢᵗ Century
Book Two

Ivan Sokolov

Soulfodder Press

Cover art by Wren Murray
Cover design by Hilary Martin
Editor Anthea Courtenay

Published April 2000 by
Soulfodder Press
Speke House
Long Beach Road
Longwell Green
Bristol, BS15 6UA, U.K.

Email: edit@soulfodder.com
Website: www.soulfodder.com -- secure orders taken

ISBN 1 903162 01 7

Printed in the United States of America by
McNaughton & Gunn Inc on acid-free recycled paper.
Typeset in ITC Souvenir Light.

God Speaks on
Family

Dedication

This book is dedicated to parents and children everywhere who have embarked on the journey of personal spiritual awakening, and are willing to abandon the current human way of fear and choose love at each moment. The words in this book have come from God and are written down by me to help you on your way. Through our journeying together and alone may we fulfil our individual and collective soul purpose.

Acknowledgements

As with any book, this one would not have been possible without help and support from many people.

Many people helped bring me to the place of readiness to dialogue with God. Most recent thanks go to Wren, Judy Crookes, Let Davidson and Rusty Myers for the part they each played in helping me assemble the pieces of my puzzle.

My thanks go to my business partners Susan Clayton and Trevor Bentley for their forbearance of me as I took a back seat in the business to focus my energies on my new direction.

My thanks to friends and acquaintances who helped make Soulfodder Press a reality to bring these words to the world, particularly Denys Laurence, Peter Andrews and numerous others who did more than they perhaps realise to inspire and motivate me to action. I offer immense appreciation to the editorial team who have worked with me, Anthea Courtenay in the UK and Roger Harrison and Margaret Harris in the USA and others who provided valuable editorial feedback.

My wife, friend, and closest companion on the spiritual path Jacquie deserves great thanks and appreciation for her belief in me, her unending support in my process of growth and the work involved in this project. She has challenged me when I have faltered, reminded me of my path when I have strayed and often provided me with my most powerful connection to God when I needed it most. Great thanks are due also to my son Joshua who, at the tender age of four when this work was written, unconsciously provided the perfect model for how to live in the present as a spiritual being having a human experience.

And my greatest thanks of all are to God for being my friend, inspirer and challenger as well as the source of the material you are about to read. May God's light shine forever upon us all.

Contents

Author's Introduction .... page 1

Introduction from God .... page 6

1   On the Family........................... page 11

2   Marriage .... page 17

3   Soul Mates .... page 24

4   Attachment and Dependency .... page 26

5   Pregnancy and Birth .... page 31

6   Children .... page 43

7   Raising Children .... page 49

8   Nature vs Nurture .... page 59

9   Education and Schooling .... page 63

10   Co-operation vs Competition .... page 71

11   Children, Toys and Violence ..... page 79

12   Emotions and Children .... page 83

13   Teenagers .... page 90

14   Rules and Controls .... page 96

15   Spiritual Education .... page 100

16   Sex and Sex Education .... page 108

17   Separation and Divorce .... page 114

18   Bereavement and Death .... page 121

19   Old Age .... page 126

20   Ancestors and Tradition .... page 131

    Epilogue .... page 137

    Notes .... page 140

    About the Author .... page 141

    Other Books in this collection .... page 142

    Companion CD and workshops .... page 146

Author's Introduction

For those who have not read **God Speaks on Life**, *let me briefly recap the introduction to that book. We will then set the scene for this one.*

In the autumn of 1998 my personal spiritual journey of many years' duration came to a crucial point of healing. Prior to that point I had explored many of the different spiritual approaches to life, from the Tao to Tibetan Buddhism, from Zen to Native American spirituality, from the Course in Miracles to Core Shamanism. All had been valuable elements of my learning and growing. None had helped me specifically heal what I felt to be the crux of my life – a strong sense of separation from God, a lack of personal connection to the Almighty.

Belief in the existence of some form of cosmic collective consciousness, some life force flowing through the universe, seemed to arise naturally out of my years of study, meditation and living. On turning forty I came to accept that my life was not one of pure chance, that I was playing out some part in an organised system in the universe that had a "centre of being" guiding it. Having been held at bay since the morning assemblies and church services of junior school, God made a definite reappearance on the scene.

In the autumn of 1998, I felt it was no longer enough to believe that God existed and could guide my life: I wanted to experience that guidance first-hand.

That experience came on 6ᵗʰ December 1998, and it transformed my life. Since that day I have been engaged in a daily dialogue with God. Each morning I write pages in my journal that include my thoughts, questions and observations about life, growth, my family and the world around me, and God's responses, observations, comments and answers.

The question that begs to be answered is who do I mean by God? Having been brought up outside any religion and devoid of a belief in the god of any church, I started life as an atheist. Then, in my twenties, I began to realise that there was too much happening to me and around me that was not explained by my scientific schooling. The pieces only seemed to fit together if a spiritual sphere existed in the universe.

You may use the name God, Allah, Jehovah, Krishna, Great Spirit or any of the countless past and present names prevalent in human society. It matters little what we call this Centre of Being. It matters little whether we refer to it as He or She, or whether we "see" it in one form or another. For me, right now, my truth is that I sit down for several hours most days and hold a conversation with God through the written word.

I know I am not the only one to have done this or to be doing it in the world today. Nor am I the only one who has been instructed by God to formulate part of our dialogue into one or more books. God told us in the introduction to **On Life** that He uses many ways to get His message across and will use as many messengers as are needed at this crucial time for humanity.

These books are being written now because we are approaching a potential crisis in the existence of our species and our planet. God wishes us to wake up to the reality of what we are creating in the world and seize the chance to change direction before it is too late. With a lot of concerted effort and a high degree of luck, we will make it. And we may not. The choice is ours. If we manage a shift away from mindless growth to conscious evolution, God will heave a sigh of relief. If we don't, another part of His Great Plan to fulfil His purpose will have collapsed. Yet this plan involves many millions of other parts and He tells us that not many tears will be shed around the wider universe for the loss of the human race.

Of the content of **On Life**, four messages stand out as most significant. They will continue to underlie nearly everything written in this and the subsequent books in this series, so I will outline them here briefly.

The Purpose of Life

God is the universe, She is all that is and all that is is part of Her. God has always been aware of Her own existence on a conceptual level, yet that was never enough. So God created the physical universe and Life within it in order that She should come to know Herself. For it is not possible to know a thing unless we know no-thing. We have to be able to get outside the one in order to observe it and come to know it experientially.

God created us all, and all the millions of living beings in the universe, on the many physical as well as spiritual planes, in order that She could experience Who She Really Is. Everything in the universe God created from Herself. We are all part of God. And this presented God and Life with a problem. If we are part of God, we are not the "other" and so cannot step outside and experience God from a different place.

For this reason, God created life in the physical realms, which would not remember being part of God. By being born into this world unaware that we are part of God, we have the opportunity to live life free from any fetters that this knowledge might impose, and so are free to experience life as different from God. It is through the experience of life and how we use that experience that we come to know God and God comes to know Herself.

Our soul purpose is to experience and discover who we really are. In the process of so doing, God can come to know Who She Really Is. In the eyes of God there is no other purpose. That is what She created the universe for.

There is only love and fear

In discussing the emotions, which God holds to be the most crucial aspects of life in the human condition, God told us in the first **God Speaks** *book that there are only two fundamental emotions in the universe, love and its opposite, fear.*

Love is the power that drives everything of value in the universe. It is the life-giving energy that flows throughout the cosmos. If we are to accept our places as spiritual children of God then we need to find ways to feel, think and act with love in all that we are and do. God is love and love is what we need to make the world go round.

Right now, we have little of it. We are living in a time and place where fear rules the day. We collude with the generation of fear throughout our societies, our communities and our families. God encourages us to change that choice and abandon fear in favour of unconditional love.

We have choice

If God, after creating us for the purpose of helping Him discover Who He Really Is, had then fixed our every thought, word and deed, our very destiny and so that of the universe, He would not be able to achieve His purpose. Just as we need to know separation from Him to come to understand what it means to be one with Him, so He needed to give us total freedom of will.

We can and do choose every moment of our lives. Nothing outside us dictates it. At every moment of joy or pain, we choose gladness or sorrow for ourselves. Every death is a suicide, a choice to put ourselves in the situation of dying: no-one can do it for us or to us.

We currently choose fear over love. We can just as easily choose love over fear and so dramatically change the world, today!

Thought is creative

Part of this process of choice entails creating our own reality. We are what we think. If we think we are born in original sin, doomed to live a life of struggle, resigned to living in fear, then that is what we create not only for ourselves but also collectively for those around us. God tells us in His first book that this process of creating reality with our thoughts happens in three ways or through some combination of them:

We can operate out of the unconscious thoughts programmed into us by our families and other meaningful adults, television, books and so on, which are absorbed in the first seven to twelve years of life.

We can operate out of the unconscious thought patterns of the society in which we live, by living out the expectations and beliefs about ourselves that stem from that society and all its hang-ups, prejudices and fears.

Or we can operate out of conscious thinking about what we want and where we are going, so choosing our thoughts and creating our future for ourselves.

What makes the third route of self-awareness so difficult to adopt is what God calls our sponsoring thoughts about ourselves. After years of personal and social conditioning these sponsoring thoughts become so ingrained in us as to oppose the conscious thoughts we may now choose. So, even whilst I choose to think that I can be successful in the world, I may also have a deeply buried sponsoring thought set up in childhood that says I will never be any good for anything. These sponsoring thoughts require to be winkled out and bathed in the love of God to be healed.

There is much else that God has to say in our first book – God Speaks on Life. *However, these four points are the most crucial to aid your understanding of the material to come. God is keen for us to get His message, so prepare for some repetition.*

The body of the book consists of God's message channelled through me. Occasional comments or questions in italics are mine. Take this material in the spirit in which it is given, with love, and make of it what you will.

As you read it, be aware that this is not the only source of direct teachings of God. Of a more conventional yet still radical stance is A Course in Miracles[1], *channelled from God in the 1970s, and much more recently,* Conversations with God[2], *books one to three, channelled through Neale Donald Walsch between 1994 and 1998. These books in particular contain much of the same philosophy as* **God Speaks** *and I would recommend you read them as well.*

Enjoy your journey, as I continue to enjoy mine.

Ivan Sokolov, summer 1999

Introduction from God

Many people struggle with the question of My identity and My form. Such is all part of the spiritual experience. To search for the meaning of life is to begin to come to terms with the essence of life. To come to terms with the essence of life is to begin to know and experience the spiritual as well as the human. To experience the spiritual is to begin to see how all life is connected. To know this total connection of life is to start to know God.

I am the life force that flows through the universe. I am the energy that gives life to all physical and spiritual forms. I am the connectedness that makes sense of the universe. I exist in all things and I exist in nothing. You might almost say I am all that there is.

In terms of human society, I am the Deity of all your religions. Some of you have chosen to represent Me in a singular, specific form, others have recognised My myriad forms of existence and given names to many gods and goddesses as representations of My parts. I am all of these and more that you may never know. I am the ultimate paradox in the universe, existing in all the disparate forms of life and in My single beingness at one and the same time.

I am God the Father, God the Son and God the Holy Ghost. The Father represents My individual existence – that which the author of this book relates to each time he sits down to write. The Son represents My presence in all the life forms that I created throughout the universe, and the Holy Ghost represents My presence as the life force, the energy that powers the universe.

And I am the Goddess – Mother and Daughter. My gender is only a projection of your humanness, not part of My essence. As such, it matters not to Me whether you relate to Me as He or She. What matters is that **you do relate to Me**.

In using the ideas and wisdom expressed in this book, you can choose to rise above the dogma that you have either taken on board or rejected and allow Me to enter your heart and mind in whatever form is easiest for you. There is no right way for us to be in relationship. There is no right way for you to perceive Me, only your way, which might be different from everyone else's. If you choose to understand the contents of this book not as My words but as the collecting together of perennial wisdom from the collective unconscious of generations of life on planet Earth, then so be it. The crucial thing is to learn from the message and live it.

It does not matter whether you believe in God or not, or what form your belief takes. If you experience life flowing through your body and connecting you to other lives around you then you are, whether you believe it or not, experiencing Me right now.

What you are going to read in this book is a message from Me to humanity. It is a message both of warning and of hope. It is a message about both personal and collective responsibility. It is a message about choice. It is a message about the need for change and how to bring it about.

Glory is potentially yours. The human race is in a position to create heaven on earth. You have the capacity to make spirit manifest in all aspects of life and know the beauty of unlimited existence. You can find ways to live together on the planet that move you all forward in terms of your spiritual evolution, stepping ever closer to fulfilling your soul purpose in life.

Humanity can be a model of how to live a physical existence in the universe. Planet Earth can be a wonderful haven of light, full of love and compassion. It can return to being the paradise it once was. All it takes is the personal will and commitment to choose love rather than fear, to recognise your spirituality as well as your humanness, to look outwards to the entire system you inhabit as well as inwards to your own soul.

The human race and planet Earth are at a critical stage in history. You face an uncertain future and there is much that you can do about it. Hear Me when I tell you that the future of human life on earth rests in your hands – you personally as well as you collectively. Each person who chooses to read this book can make a difference.

What is the uncertainty in your future? You have reached a point in human social and technical development where life on earth is already unsustainable. That means that, if you continue just as you are, it will not be possible for you to live out your natural lifespan.

Taking action to change things requires you to **want to change**. It requires you to decide that the possibly quite considerable discomfort of personal and social change is preferable to the lack of a future for you and your children. Above all it requires you to love yourselves enough to want to survive. It requires you to love life enough to want to see it continue in all its potential glory.

Planet Earth is fast approaching a point of re-organisation. Some of you have recently come to realise that the world on which you live and all life thereon form one physical and spiritual ecosystem. Human life is only one small part of that system, yet humankind has had a disproportionate influence over the whole. Your influence in the last one hundred years has been increasingly detrimental. Humanity has been degrading the quality of life on Earth not only for yourselves but also for all other life forms. You have taken upon yourselves the roles of judge, jury and executioners of thousands if not hundreds of thousands of species. You have taken upon yourselves the roles of judge and jury of human life – and now the role of executioner is close to being played out.

Humankind's lack of full awareness and understanding of the deep spiritual connection between every element of existence has brought you and your home to the brink of destruction.

You now have the choice. You can sit back and let the ravages continue through to the bitter end, or you can take action to turn things around before it is too late.

Sitting back and taking no action will lead to the ever-increasing degradation of your physical and social environment. It will lead to greater frequency of natural "disasters" as the systems of the planet struggle to maintain a balance. It will lead to ever-mounting levels of fear in the human psyche which will result in violence on scales you have not seen before. It will lead to a point when the ecosystem of which you are but a part decides that it has had enough. Gaia will readjust herself to slough off the irritant on her skin, and humankind, living as you know it now, will be gone.

My message contained in these books is designed to help you realise the potential of what you can be, what is not working and what needs to change. It is designed to help you make the changes now, before it is too late.

It all starts with personal choice. Making the choice to question life as it now is. Making the choice to hear My message. Making the choice to take it in and act on it. Making the choice to accept the help that I offer you through these books.

What have you got to lose? Only life on earth.

Some will ask how come I am speaking to you in this way at this time? I choose this time to speak because I love you all and do not wish to see you choose to destroy yourselves. I choose this way to speak to you as I am choosing other unconventional ways, because too few of you choose to hear me directly yourselves. Accept my love for you and listen to what I have to say. Then you will at least be better informed to make the choices that face you.

Through the **God Speaks** collection I am proposing a real revolution in the way you lead your lives. If you wish to ensure that you can continue to live on planet Earth for the foreseeable future, then revolution is needed **now**. It is not likely to come from those in positions of power and authority. They have already had to sacrifice too much of their humanness and their spirituality in climbing to the top to be able to recognise the truth that is staring them in the face. What is needed is a decision to be made by thousands of millions of people throughout your planet that enough is enough, that the time has come to revert to being **homo sapiens** rather than **homo technicus** running out of control, and so fulfil your spiritual destiny.

1. On the Family

The family structure is vitally important to humanity at the present time. Families provide people with a safe, supportive environment in which to learn and grow. They can be the seat of spiritual evolution for humanity, a source of unconditional love that can also spread out into wider communities. Families have the potential to be immensely nurturing of the body, mind and spirit. You learn most of what you need to know about life from your experiences in and of the family. This gives parents both huge power and considerable responsibility to ensure that they provide their children with the best possible start in life.

Unfortunately, families in your society have come under increasing pressure in modern times and do not always manage to fulfil the promise that they hold. This does not mean that they should be replaced with some other structure. The family, in one form or another, will continue to be a powerful tool for socialisation for many years to come, even as the detail of that socialisation will change.

In this book we will consider many elements of family life and the raising of your young. All that we will say will sit within the current concepts of family, aiming to show you how the process of raising a family can become part of moving you all forward towards the future that beckons you.

Most of what I have to tell you relates to family life of any shape or size, whether nuclear, single-parent, extended, blended or any other label you may attach to it. Before we can consider all these different forms of family life, it would be useful to consider what role the family can play in the spiritual development of individuals, and so of the human race as a whole.

In **On Life** I have already written on the subject of sex, lovemaking and spirituality. You have the potential to combine the profound physical pleasure of sex with the process of experiencing the flow of My Love through you to each other and the world, as well as to the physical creation of a new human life ready for the incarnation of a soul on your planet. This is the most wondrous process and one that will remain central to the human condition for all time.

If undertaken with the reverence that it deserves as a true spiritual channel of love, the result is a bond between a man and a woman with that which is waiting to be born and which becomes the child of their love. The current human social unit best suited to this process is the long-term, loving relationship between two humans of each sex. From this ideal perspective, any family that is raising children within it will be most effective if it contains a father and mother joyfully sharing their roles as parents. This does not mean that other families do not work. There are many single parents and same-sex couples doing a good job of guiding children through their early years.

Let us stick with the ideal for a moment, however. There is much to be said for this ideal family to include quite a lot more than just mum and dad and 2.4 kids. An enormous amount of the stresses and strains experienced in "civilised" societies stems from the pressure felt by parents living in isolated nuclear families with little or no help or support from networks such as their families of origin, their friends or communities.

Traditional communities that have a wider definition of family find it very much easier to cope with the stresses and strains of life. At their widest, families in some social contexts include virtually the whole tribe or community, with next to no-one excluded from a sense of kinship with the children of any particular couple. Such is the wisdom of this way of thinking and behaving that you will find it in place in most highly evolved societies across the universe.

None of this makes nuclear families, whether with one parent or two, in any way wrong or second-rate. Yet they will find the task they face far harder to achieve in the absence of support. In the case of families in which, for whatever reason, only one parent is active in the process of loving and guiding children, the children will inevitably receive less to help them in their growing up than if they have two loving adults on hand. A family which includes two adults, one of whom is not a biological parent, will be able to provide more for the children emotionally and spiritually provided that the non-biological parent is aware enough to love the children unconditionally.

In families in which two or more adults of the same gender share the task of guiding children lovingly, the children will have the potential to gain more than where there is only one. Yet, not having a balance of male and female energy present will detract from the total they might otherwise get

In considering all forms of family, let me remind you that there are no such things as right and wrong in My Universe. Some things work and some don't. I do not condemn. If you were to stop condemning yourselves and others your world would be a happier, saner and safer place to live in.

Let us briefly say something here about the difference between judging and condemning. It is important for you to become effective at making judgments in your lives based on as much information as you can uncover. This ability to discern as accurately as possible, moment to moment, whether things are working, whether situations and people serve you well and what the possible outcomes might be is a crucial skill for all of you to develop. It is unfortunate that it becomes entangled with your readiness to condemn those things, people and circumstances that you judge as negative or not useful. This is such a prevalent tendency that in the English language judging someone has become almost synonymous with condemning them. Be as discerning as you possibly can. Do not sit in judgment waiting to hand out condemnation or commendation, punishment or reward.

In our first book we touched briefly on the idea that the people best suited to bear children are not necessarily those best equipped to guide them through the process of growing up. Physically it is easier and safer for young adults to conceive and bear children than it is for older ones. Both the man and woman have been exposed to fewer polluting substances and energies, so their reproductive systems are likely to be most healthy in the first ten years of their sexually mature life.

However, those first ten years, and probably the following ten or more, are the years when they are likely to be least suited to spending time at home passing on the wisdom of the species to new members. For a start, they have not finished their own learning and growing process, so may be far from wise themselves. They are normally the people most suited to be out in the world undertaking the physically and emotionally strenuous activities that your society demands.

In many more highly evolved societies in the universe, young adults procreate the next generation and leave the bulk of caring and education to their elders. The elders are both better equipped for this task and less for that of working in the world. Such a system exists to some degree amongst a few tribal cultures of your indigenous peoples who have escaped the process of "civilisation".

I do not wish to glorify traditional tribal cultures on your planet, yet there are those that compare favourably with highly evolved societies in other parts of the universe in this particular regard. Those effective societies which have been fortunate enough to retain their tribal way of life have many advantages over the "advanced" societies which have struggled to make their communities civilised places to live in. They have avoided growing larger and so have retained a way of life more akin to an extended family than an unrelated community.

Such societies I observe to be humanly and spiritually better suited to supporting young human beings in growing to maturity than those in which the vast majority of you live. They work: yours don't. There is much I can tell you of what I observe that is not working in the nature and process of "family", particularly in your westernised societies. I do not condemn the family as an institution, just as I do not condemn anything else about life in the universe or on planet Earth. And, in this book we will consider many ways in which you can all make the family work far more effectively for you, your children and the human race as a whole.

For families are not just about raising children. They can also be about deepening the spiritual bonds between people who have decided to follow the same life path for a time. They can provide a haven for the elders of society, not to mention the wounded and damaged members who are too often now left to fend for themselves in a seemingly loveless world.

Families can evolve to play a vital role in the evolution of society, if you are willing to take up the challenge.

2. Marriage

As we said in the previous chapter, the bond of love and creativity that holds two people in a committed relationship is the most effective foundation for the family. Such a bond is currently most normally described as marriage. It can equally be found in any relationship where the partners enter into a commitment to live, love and grow together.

The level of commitment you normally associate with marriage provides the potential for an environment in which two people can support each other's personal and spiritual development. It can be the place of complete unconditional love, where you need have no fears about being accepted as who you really are, warts and all. It can be the relationship in which you experiment with finding out your soul purpose in life and support each other to achieve that which brought you to this world in the first place. The loving bond of two people sharing domestic aspects of their lives can be strong enough to withstand the fear and envy that can otherwise so easily come between friends as you change and grow.

And, right now, marriage as an institution is not unlike the family itself. For some it is a glorious, happy and spirit-filled experience, whilst for others it is more akin to a term of imprisonment. Inevitably, marriage is what you make of it. Certainly in the West, and increasingly in other parts of the world, marriage as an institution is not fulfilling its promises.

At this time in the life of humanity, that is completely appropriate. As a species, you are going through a transition and most of the ways in which you do things need to change. Marriage and the family are no exception. Marriages are breaking up all around you because the model on which you base them no longer works.

You are firmly trapped in a potential conflict between society's need for marriage and the needs of the individuals within marriage. Society has contributed to the process of reducing the size of the family to the nuclear unit, which emotionally – and maybe even financially – is not really viable in your world of change and turmoil. As we said in Chapter One, families consisting of young parents and children are the least effective places in which to raise the next generation. They are also the least effective places for the emotional and spiritual maturing of the young married couple. The lack of the wisdom and maturity that traditionally resides in the eldest generation of the family has its effect on both the adults and the children of a young marriage.

Society needs two young adults to stay together for the sake of the children, living in one economic unit, which in reality is not emotionally viable. Society needs this because it has not yet accepted the challenge of harnessing the potential for self-responsibility to the practice of shared responsibility for all.

If you were all aware that you are one with each other, that you are all one with Me and every aspect of the universe you see and experience, then taking personal responsibility for your lives would also mean sharing responsibility for each other's. You could only live in an equitable society where what was required for a decent standard of living was shared amongst everyone worldwide. In such a global caring society the family would not need to exist as a unit of economic production and consumption. Then, instead of families growing smaller, as they have over the last couple of generations, they could be more akin to the tribes of the more spiritually advanced peoples of the universe.

In the context of the family as tribe, marriage would serve a different purpose.

IS: And, right now and for the foreseeable future, I can't see that happening for most of us on planet Earth. So I wonder if we shouldn't focus more on what needs to shift within current reality.

If you cannot see such profound changes happening on your planet in the future, if you cannot fore-see them, then they are not likely ever to happen. By holding such changes in your fore-sight, you can move a long way towards creating that reality with the power of your thoughts. If you give up before you start, you are accepting the negativity of your thoughts and so will create the negative reality that you are thinking. It requires so little of each individual to change the future beyond will and foresight. The combined power of billions of individuals using their will, choosing something different today, would bring about instant change.

Back to marriage.

There is nothing sacred about the union of a man and a woman in matrimony, whatever the Christian churches tell you. If you can successfully unravel the web of expectations, promises and fears that engulfs the emotional, sexual and spiritual union of two people who want to journey together for a while on your planet, then marriage can be a profound experience. If you wrap it up in unrealistic promises, social taboos and legal red tape, you risk making the whole process more of a spell in prison than a great life adventure.

To be truly successful, a marriage needs to be lived in the here and now. In **On Life** we spoke about time only really existing in the present. Live your commitment to your life partner today, right now to the full. Be with them, share yourself with them, love and play with them in the reality of your mutual commitment to the moment.

Free yourself up from the sense that this has to be forever, and you are more likely to make it last. Most marriages fall apart precisely because they are all tied up in the first place and the couple are not living their lives in genuine partnership, growing and changing together joyfully. There is a huge danger in the marriage promise – indeed, in any promise that you make for the long term. In truth, about the only thing you can promise is that tomorrow will not be the same as today, and tomorrow you will not be the same as you are today.

Human beings have a tendency to want to hold on to the present as it becomes the past refusing to accept the evidence of continual growth and change. You adopt all sorts of unuseful patterns of being and doing to reinforce the belief that you won't, and indeed can't, change. It is one of the greatest lies that you live.

It is this fundamental lie that makes a mockery of the promise of "till death us do part".

To make a promise that you will stay together and love each other forever, regardless of the inevitability that you will both change, does not work. What does work is to make a promise to grow and change together today, and see what the morrow will bring. You can thus approach marriage as a partnership on a journey of adventure, in full recognition that you will individually and collectively change as you proceed, knowing that you can cope with those changes by adapting your way of being together or, if need be, even deciding to separate and pursue different journeys.

That is the loving way to enter into a commitment. That is the way best suited to creating a small element of emotional stability in a constantly changing world. This can then provide a basis for the growth of the next generation, secure not in its fixedness but in its flexibility and resilience.

The other great benefit of marriage as partnering **through** life rather than **for** life is that it removes the element of possession and ownership that can be so insidious in the forms of the institution you have today. Replace "my husband/wife" with "the man/woman I am journeying through life with" and you immediately open more space in the relationship for love and spirit. You take away huge areas in which jealousy can spring up. You remove the sense of a right to control or demand. You establish an equality in the adventure and a recognition that being a partner to someone through life is an active, doing role as well as a being role. Marriage as partnership requires work and play. It requires a commitment to grow and learn together, rather than taking your spouse for granted simply because they are married to you.

IS: And what of the situations where some would say that the partnership is not equal, when one person in the marriage stays home and doesn't contribute to the income?

This can only be an issue seen from an economic perspective. Life as a whole needs to be seen from all possible perspectives; viewing it from only one will always distort the picture and present you with unreal conclusions.

If both parties to this partnership live their lives to the full, emotionally and spiritually, then they will always be equal in their humanness. It will not matter what one does for a living, or how well qualified (and thus well paid) one may be compared with the other. In a truly civilised world it would not be possible to value an investment banker, heart surgeon, pop star, film actress or any other highly paid role above that of full-time carer and parent. This is a really important attitude for you to change. And the place to start is in the mind of every person who currently thinks that what they do is more important than what anyone else does.

Let us continue to play with the comparisons between partnership and marriage. With the best will in the world, you establish a marriage by making vows, maybe even "holy vows", in the false belief that I so decree it. As we have said, the promises thus made are in reality likely to be lies, because you cannot know that you can keep them unless you lie to yourself about the changes that happen day by day inside you.

By contrast, most working partnerships start with an agreement to work together, which is then regularly reviewed and renewed. Such agreements usually outline how the parties will work together, how the rewards will be divided up, and who will be responsible for what. They would also benefit enormously from going a stage further and outlining what is important to the parties – the values and principles in the here and now by which they will live, work and play. These, too, will benefit from regular review and updating as the partners grow and change.

Many partnership agreements are only drawn up for a short period, say one year at a time. Within the context of a family, two partners may agree to extend aspects of the partnership at least to cover the period of dependency of their children.

In an ideal framework, think what could be achieved by including within that partnership the wider family roles that will be interdependent with the "married couple" and their children. There is no reason why a marital partnership agreement could not be rewritten on the birth of a child to include the grandparents. It could even be expanded to form an agreement between the pairing adults and the other members of the tribal-style community amongst whom they live, work and play.

IS: What about situations such as open marriages, adultery, and the many people who choose not to get married at all?

Those who choose not to stand in front of some official, be it of church or state, and speak the prescribed vows are either saying them in private or perhaps already moving towards a concept of partnership not dissimilar from that which we are talking about here.

As to open marriages, I think this question is addressed by what I have said above. If you can do away with the sense of possession that is so prevalent in your marriages today, and find an equality of relating at an emotional and spiritual level, then you will either not want an open marriage or will freely negotiate one between you. The choice is yours. I am not going to condemn you one way or another.

In all of this as well as with the issue of adultery, remember your real purpose in life and constantly ask the question "How far does my behaviour reflect **who I really am**?" A life spent lovingly in pursuit of discovering who you really are in the universe and how to express that will be a life well lived. Relationships lived lovingly in pursuit of your soul purpose will be relationships of a spiritual nature.

3. Soul Mates

It is certainly true that you can and do experience relationships with people in this life whom you have met before in other lives. Souls met in one incarnation or in the spiritual realm may well choose to play a role in each other's physical lives as a way of helping each other to achieve the greater purpose of their spiritual existence.

I understand that many people who use the term "soul mate" do so to mean the ideal lover, the person so well suited to be their companion that they must have a strong soul connection with them. This is a somewhat romantic view of how life unfolds. Unfortunately, the person you consider to be your ideal life partner in this incarnation may not always be doing your soul the greatest favour by being in your life. They may be colluding with your wish to lead a tranquil life of human ease which moves you no further forward in the great discovery of your soul journey. They may not be being a very good mate to your soul at all.

It is certainly possible for you to have in your partner an aspect of the same soul that has been your human partner in other lives. You may choose to continue to pair up on planet Earth because you can offer each other a level of soul support and challenge which surpasses that which you could each get from someone else.

If you broaden the use of the term "soul mates" to include strongly connected soul aspects that are repeatedly part of your human life, then you can begin to see that some of your closest "mates" are not necessarily the ones you choose as partners in any of your lives. The apparent thorn in your side who repeatedly engineers for you to face up to lessons unlearnt may be even more your soul mate than your husband, wife or lover.

You might question how useful a concept this is. To what extent does it serve you to focus your attention on only one or two people as being "special" to you in some way? It might be that the greatest favour in your personal spiritual journey is done to you by someone you barely know, yet whose life has in some way touched yours and left you profoundly changed. They may have been the best mate to your soul you have ever had, and you may not even know their name.

This opens up the possibility of a different definition. Instead of thinking in terms of a mate at the level of soul, that is a friend your soul has encountered before, how about thinking of the people who are now or have been a mate to your soul, those who befriend you at the spiritual level in this life but who may have had no soul connection with you before and will have none again.

Rather than searching desperately for your "soul mate", recognise the human and spiritual mates you have around you right now. Who knows, the very person you seek with such longing may already be in your life, if you would just be prepared to remove the surface layer of romance and rethink what a soul mate would be for you. In this way, you might then find the mates that your soul could do with in this life. You might also find a loving partner for this moment in Universal Time.

4. Attachment and Dependency

Being human is a process of interdependent living. At a soul level you are all part of the same life force in the universe, so totally interconnected as to be one. And there is a very great difference between connection and dependence. The need some of you have to be emotionally dependent on another human being stems precisely from your inability to accept that you are not alone. It is through your experience of loneliness, your separation from Me, that you crave attachment to each other.

When your desire for closeness comes from such success at loving yourself that you have enormous spare capacity to lavish on others, then you can form beautiful interdependent relationships of great intimacy, trust and mutual respect. In such relationships, attachment will not be an issue. You will be free to stay precisely because you are free to go.

When your desire for closeness comes from a need to feel safe **in** the other you are likely to form attachments that are not useful, which lead to dependency. Failing to find the wholeness inside you, you search for ways to feel whole in relationship to another. When you find a potential fit, you will inevitably attach to it, holding on in a dependent way for fear of losing your false sense of wholeness and security.

An alternative would be to seek a degree of safety in your relationship **with** the other, where a mutual interdependence can provide for you both without undue risk of attachment.

Your strength comes from the spiritual not the human side. Seek for wholeness through the aspect of your soul incarnated in your being. When you can open yourself to Me and the aspects of your soul that exist on other spiritual planes, you will no longer need attachments to human beings or earthly things. Then you will be free to enjoy all that is human without any dependence.

How do we break out of the attachments we already have? Many intimate relationships appear to "work" just because the attachment is mutual. When one side begins to change, the dependency issues can become hugely difficult for both to deal with.

Nobody holds on tighter than the person who thinks they are about to fall.

It is true that some of you ignore the inner journey to find yourselves and a spiritual peace for as long as you can. When it comes, the resulting rocking of the boat can cause enormous pain and recriminations. In this avoidance, you do yourself, your partner and many others in your life a disservice.

Accepting that the time has come to break free of attachments and regain your emotional independence is a brave and necessary step to spiritual growth. If you can do it with a high degree of unconditional love, you will be able to find ways to minimise the pain on all sides. Recognise and acknowledge that the old ways fulfilled a valid, if misguided, purpose. Starting from the basis that you were doing the best you knew how, given your past experience and present circumstances, you can examine how you can better meet the need for relating other than by being dependent.

Fear is what gets in the way. If you are the one who realises that the time has come to break out of your emotional attachment, you are likely to experience fear of being trapped, fear of having your new-found awareness denied and fear of being submerged by the emotional pain of your partner not wanting to let go.

For your partner, the fear of loss may be almost overwhelming if he or she is not ready to look inside to find himself or herself within the relationship.

Unfortunately, the fear can be so strong that the tendency is to withdraw from the other, creating a vicious circle of increased fear of loss, and so on.

The only thing that can help in such a fearful situation is unconditional love. Ideally you will reach a point where you can genuinely announce to the world that you love yourself enough to want to change, that you love your partner enough to want to help them change, and that you love your relationship enough to want to stay in it and transform it into something that will feed you both and still have love left over to feed those around you.

Minimise the risk of your partner feeling fear of loss by moving closer towards them, not further away. Find it in your heart to want to stop being dependent and depended upon, at the same time as wanting to love and be loved even more deeply.

For most people, this will require help from outside. Spiritual counselling or emotional counselling from spiritually aware helpers will make the process of shifting from dependence to interdependence infinitely easier. The fear and pain can be replaced by joy and pleasure as both sides come to see just how much more they can get from a spiritual relationship between lovers of the self as well as of the other.

Nothing is hard to put into practice that comes from a loving place. Only when you succumb to fear do things become difficult. Love is the ultimate facilitator, fear the ultimate block.

I would not suggest that anyone try to work this way on their own as their very first venture into a spiritual way of being. The chances are that they and their partner will be carrying too much baggage from the past to find it easy to be this loving and accepting. If your dependent relationship is already coming apart, then you might be wise to leave it gracefully. You have time enough to work on the implications for your personal journey before you enter into another one.

If you do manage to work together on breaking the dependency without breaking the relationship, what you end up with will be well worth the effort. A non-attached bond of love is a remarkable thing.

Is there is a connection between issues of dependency in marriages and adult relationships and early childhood experiences?

The connection will not always be simple, yet a connection will usually exist. In the industrialised western world, children are expected to become independent well in advance of their physical, emotional and spiritual readiness. Forced breaking of the dependence on the mother is very likely to be a significant factor in the failure to develop a secure sense of self in the child. It is this lack of an adequate sense of self and personal safety that usually leads to the need to be dependent on another adult throughout life.

It is very natural for a child to retain the need to be emotionally dependent on the primary carer, usually the mother, until he or she reaches the age of full readiness to venture out into the world. This is seldom much in advance of six or seven, and may take as long as ten or more years for some children.

We will talk more about this when we consider schooling and child care in the coming chapters. Suffice it to say that a considerable relaxation of the need for very young children to be independent would eliminate the problems of over-dependence in marriage for many adults. Your current pattern of sending four- and five-year-old children out of the home into a crowded environment, lacking in the total love and attention that one or more full-time carers can provide, is not an effective one.

5. Pregnancy and Birth

The process of growing the human foetus and its delivery into the outside world is one of the great miracles of human life. For the mother it is both a great sacrifice and a great privilege. A sacrifice because of the physical strains she will experience and the disruption required in everyday life for so long. A privilege because of the joy that can result and the never-ending gifts that motherhood can bring into a woman's life for years to come.

It can also be a significant element in a woman's spiritual journey. You might almost say that a built-in side effect of the whole process of bearing a baby and subsequently caring for an infant is to open the heart and soul of the mother to total unconditional love. Not everyone will choose to experience the spiritual transformation this process offers, yet many will know that their ability to love has been increased as a result. The incarnating child is as close to Me as it is possible for most human beings to get. As such, caring for it provides both mother and father with the opportunity to open a channel directly to My love. Even during the pregnancy it is very possible for the parents to start to connect spiritually with their child, through their child to Me and, at the same time, ever more deeply with each other.

Growing in the mother's womb is also an important process of spiritual transformation for the child. Through the safety, comfort and nourishment of her body she provides the unborn child with an environment in which it can start the process of transition from spirit to matter. This is such an important time in this quite drawn out process. A loving mother able to take the time to feel connected with her unborn child can do a great deal to welcome the new human being into its body, easing what is a potentially harsh move from the world of spirit into physical form. During this time she can do much to soothe the incarnating soul, making friends with it, and talking it through the early days of its life in the womb.

What part does karma play in all of this?

The difficulty with the concept of karma as it is often understood in your world is that it contains an element of judgment and punishment. You do something "bad" in one life and are punished for it in the next life. This presupposes that the universe is a judgmental place ruled by a harsh, unforgiving God. It is not and I am not.

The incarnating soul chooses many aspects of the life it will lead by virtue of the physical body and earthly context into which it is born. It does so in order to have the experiences it needs in the physical world to live out its purpose of rediscovering **who it really is**, and so remembering itself as one with Me. There are many lessons about life that can usefully be learnt in the journey of coming to full awareness and accepting that love is all there is and that you are all one with each other and with Me.

For some people those lessons may be easier to learn if they choose a life with some level of physical or mental affliction. For some they may be easier if they choose harsh circumstances in their families or communities and the social and political environment around them.

Each of you has your own personal path to follow. Many of you do not manage to follow it fully as chosen when you incarnate because you get sucked into the powerful creative forces of collective thought processes and forget what you have come to learn. This is a large part of why you choose to keep coming back, in the belief that next time you will be better able to fulfil your learning and so come nearer to achieving your purpose in life.

Karma in the sense of paying for the sins of a past life in this one does not exist in the universal nature of things that I created, any more than do heaven or hell. And you may well have chosen to live a life this time round based on what your soul believes it needs to learn as a result of other lives lived or being lived right now in the physical realms.

Does that mean that a child that dies in the womb or at birth has learnt what it came into this physical manifestation to learn?

It may mean that, and it may not. Sometimes a soul will choose to incarnate for the benefit of another rather than itself. The unborn child may choose to incarnate to help with the healing of the mother or father it has chosen. If this requires the death of the physical body prior to birth then that soul willingly lets go and returns to spirit. It may be that the soul recognises that the context into which it has chosen to be born is not suited to the life lessons it wishes to learn this time round and so chooses to leave the body before it is fully developed.

These ideas will be hard to accept by people who see human life as sacred. It is not. It is the life of the soul that is sacred, for it was created by Me. The soul willingly moves in and out of the physical form without any sense of trauma. Life never ends or begins, it is a continuous process of living; only the physical context changes, the garage for the soul is periodically knocked down and rebuilt. It is only those who watch from the physical realm who see the beginning of life in conception and its ending in death. If you recognise this as an illusion, then you will no longer be afraid of death and will be better able to live to the full in the moment of now.

This does not negate the importance of the body. The growth of the foetus during pregnancy is about the most important period in the physical development of the child. It is well known by doctors that many of the seeds of vitality are sown during these nine months of growth. This is when the unborn body is most at risk from pollutants, inadequate nutrition, unnecessary stimulants or sedatives. Much has been documented about the physical process of human foetal growth, clarifying lots of opportunities to ensure that every child born into this world has a good biochemical basis for all future physical growth.

It is worth every effort a mother can make to provide herself with an excellent diet leading up to and during pregnancy. The less contaminated the food and drink she takes in the less harm she will pass on to her child. Unfortunately, the list of irritants that can affect the physical and emotional systems of the human body is very long. The food most mothers eat contains residues of pesticides, herbicides and fertilisers. As a result of the agro-chemical farming systems you now employ it is also lacking both in minute elements of biochemical makeup and in the vitality of unpolluted living food. The expanding trend towards organic production will make it easier for you to ensure a full and adequate natural diet for women carrying babies.

You need to be aware that the list of potential pollutants is not limited to food alone. I want you to be aware of the ways in which the life you lead right now potentially interferes with your desire to provide your children with a good start. I am aware that in doing so, I am at risk of exposing you to unpalatable truths that some may not wish to hear.

The air you breathe is full of chemical pollutants that can affect many of the bodily functions of the mother carrying a child, and can be passed through her blood to the child itself, affecting the growth of nerve and brain tissue, bone structure and internal organs. All these effects are so minute as to be discounted by medical science at this stage of human development. Yet the end result is to weaken the elements of a finely balanced system that would otherwise be able to function almost indefinitely.

Some of the air pollution you expose yourselves to comes directly from the waste products carried in the air from cars, factories, power stations, incinerators, even the back-garden bonfire burning apparently organic rubbish. More of it comes from the materials you surround yourselves with – the plaster and paint on your walls, the unnatural fibres in your floor and furniture coverings, not to mention your clothes and the residue from the chemicals you use to treat your clothes, your hair and your skin – the list is long.

Then there is the pollution of sound and energy that is so all-pervasive in your modern world. Just as people are now beginning to discover the healing power of sound, so you could usefully explore the polluting power of sound, the power to affect the vibrations of molecular structures and so bring about changes in the working of cells which are not conducive to the truly healthy growth of the human body and mind.

You have also filled your planetary airwaves with a

myriad electro-magnetic radiations, any one element of which has the capacity to effect shifts in the vibration of core aspects of the life process, not just for you, but also for every living thing on the planet – indeed the very structure of the planet itself. You have to travel a long way from "civilisation" to escape the radiation caused by electricity flowing through cables, by radio and television receivers and transmitters, by the electrical energy being generated and expended through cars, trucks, boats, planes and trains. The use of mobile phones has added a shockingly dangerous element to the equation, bathing whole countries in high frequency radio waves which you will one day realise are detrimental to your own health and the health of all life.

What can be done I hear you ask?

You live in uncomfortable times. Humankind has succumbed to a fear-based mentality that ostensibly pushes on and on for "progress", whilst actually taking you backwards on the path from achieving your individual and collective purpose in life.

Yet there is much that you can each begin to do to reclaim responsibility for cleaning up the world. Educate yourselves as to the risks you face and know that you can choose to avoid many of them. Paradoxically it is the richer and more "developed" societies that face the greatest threats in these areas. You can avoid many pollutants once you know of their existence. You can choose to furnish and decorate your houses with natural materials and products. You can be selective about the music you expose yourselves and your children to.

You can change the values you live by. Right now, you are at risk of valuing convenience over good health, speed over quality, and money over long-term survival.

Do away with the cordless phones that save you having to get up from your chairs and be willing to return to having fewer telephones in the house if you cannot give them up at all.

Do away with the need to be instantly in touch with anyone, anywhere and give up your mobile phones.

Simplify the electronic gadgetry in your homes and offices and be willing to take the extra time required to cook a meal rather than microwave it, write a letter by hand rather than use a word-processor.

So many of your technological advances are not advances for the human body, soul or mind at all.

I appreciate that this will be hard for many of you. Life appears to be much easier surrounded by gadgetry. How realistic is it to ask people to care for their health and vitality? How realistic is it to ask people to care for the environment and the other forms of life with which you share this world? You have choice in all these things. Right now, the human race is choosing technological progress over human evolution. It has chosen that road before and almost destroyed itself completely.

The technology is different this time, but it is also true that you have not learnt the lessons of the last global catastrophe – that technology can be used as a servant of the spiritual process of life on earth, but not as the master of the physical. I will not say more here other than telling you to heed the warning and wake up to the reality you are creating individually and collectively. Much has been written about the fall of Atlantis, which you can study to begin to grasp some of what happened all those thousands of years ago.

This revelation has profound consequences for what we are doing in the world.

Everything we write here has equally profound consequences for what you are doing in the world. Much of it has been revealed before and humankind has not taken adequate notice. There is a risk that only a minority of people will take notice now, as the truth is revealed again. Part of our work is to reach enough people who do not feel totally disempowered by your ways of living and to help them to believe they can make a difference and contribute to the shift that is starting to gain momentum. It is not too late. Rest assured that, depressing as the situation now seems, many people are beginning to make a difference around the world.

Let us return to pregnancy and birth. We have dealt so far with the physical aspect. Now let us also consider the importance of emotional and mental. Electro-magnetic radiation is not the only type of vibration the unborn child is exposed to. He or she is also exposed continually, and more significantly, to the emotional and mental vibrations of the mother and other people around, whether or not they are involved in the caring process. It is as important to be aware of the thoughts and feelings the unborn child is exposed to as it is to take into account the physical. A child growing inside its mother's womb, surrounded by love and positive affirmations about it and the life it can look forward to, will have a head start over the child growing in a fearful or rejecting atmosphere.

Many of you are in such denial of the power of the human heart and mind that you place both unborn and growing children in fields of fear and negativity, oblivious to the detrimental effect it has on them. Mother and father, and even older siblings and grandparents, can make up for the times when this cannot be avoided by creating extended moments to just be quietly with the new family member in the womb. Sit with and talk to the incarnating child, tell it how much it is loved, how welcome it is in your family, what a lot it has to look forward to in life. Sing to it, include it in family life as much as is possible. A new baby is a member of the family from the moment it imbeds into the lining of the womb.

It would be useful to be more aware both of your own emotional and mental processes and of the effect these have on a growing foetus. You could then make a conscious choice as to whether to conceive a child in the first place in full awareness of the many issues we have briefly outlined here. For many of the human race, the process of procreation has become so automatic that conscious choice has all but disappeared.

The time of planning to conceive a child would appropriately be one of careful review of all aspects of the parents' personal states, family context, financial and environmental situations, all designed to answer the heartfelt question, "Is the time right for us to enter on this life-long commitment to bring another being into the world?" If this question were now asked genuinely by every couple of childbearing age on the planet, the majority would probably answer no! Not only would you solve your problems of population growth, you would also have a chance to bring up more spiritually aware and less damaged children than you do now.

There are organisations in the world that encourage women to prepare their bodies for pregnancy, suggesting dietary and lifestyle guidelines.

They would be even better placed to help if they were taking a far more holistic and spiritual approach to the issues they are dealing with. It is so very important to consider the spiritual as well as the physical, mental and emotional. If you would put the spiritual first, then the emotional, mental and physical would naturally follow on. If you understood your soul purpose and had the spiritual and emotional awareness to appreciate what you are now doing to your physical systems, you would not be able to continue acting as you are.

The birth process is a significant marker in the lives of a child, its parents and the wider family that ideally contains them all. On the face of it there are wondrous things that your society has done to make it a "safer" process, in which fewer babies and their mothers die. Compared with what you often refer to as "the dark ages" of pre-scientific medicine, things have improved on the purely physical level. But you have paid quite a price for the improvements.

The price you have paid is, once again, the loss of the spiritual and emotional elements of the experience. In a few current cultures and in distant times when generations of women were involved in the celebration of the beginning of life, the process was more open to spirit and heart than it is in your westernised hospitals surrounded by doctors and nurses. And as a truly holistic process, the success rate was as high if not at times higher than today. A successful birth was more about the choice of the incarnating child than the process itself; after all, some children were not meant to be born at all. Their experience of conception and pregnancy being the lesson they chose this time round.

What about birth control and abortion?

Birth control can only be an issue in a society that sees a purely limited role for the human sexual act, that of procreation. As we wrote in Book One, if this were the case, I might have more efficiently designed the human female body to ripen for pregnancy once a year or even less frequently. As it is, the human sexual act has built into it the capacity to be the finest process of enabling love to flow that it is possible to imagine, not just between two people but also outwards to those around them. Familiarise yourselves with what I said in the chapter on Sex and Love-making in **God Speaks on Life**. The womb has two functions, physical and spiritual; it not only provides a place for the foetus to grow, it also provides a channel into the physical world of My love energy.

In the instinctive knowledge that this is so, human beings have practised birth control for millennia, so freeing the woman from the risk of unwanted pregnancy. It is only in recent historical times that this has changed. It was a change brought about by the rise in power of the churches, who wished to retain the connection with God within their own power and control, and not acknowledge it as possible within every simple act of lovemaking. In some churches' insistence that sex is only for procreation and that birth control is "wrong", much of the natural understanding of contraception has been lost by women in many parts, though not all, of the world.

To do anything other than advocate a return to a common understanding and awareness of the process of human birth control and its value on planet Earth does not make much sense at the stage you have reached in the overcrowding of your home.

As to abortion: this point has already been answered in this chapter, and I repeat: human life is not sacred in the eyes of God. Nor is it meant to be needlessly wasted or abused. The question each individual can most usefully address is how far their actions contribute to their discovery and expression of who they really are? And remember two things: one is that you cannot take another person's human life away from them without their consent. The second is that Life is never-ending and is not unduly affected by the ending of your time in this physical body.

If considered necessary, abortion needs to be carried out with full awareness. The awareness needs to be both of the soul needs of the unborn child and of the life-long emotional consequences for the mother, and the father where appropriate. The termination of a human life in the womb, undertaken with full loving awareness, need not be traumatic for either child or mother.

Yet how much more loving and effective it would be to act with such awareness and self-responsibility that pregnancy does not occur unnecessarily in the first place. Choice is always there to be taken.

6. Children

As critical as the pregnancy and birth process is for the holistic health of the newborn child, the energy expended by parents in the next eighteen years dwarfs the amount of time and energy that usually goes into those first nine months. Much of the content of this book focuses on aspects of raising and educating children. Before we make a start in that direction, let us look more generally at the subject of children.

It is common for society to set an arbitrary age boundary around the definition of children, which is not entirely valid. After all, you are all someone's child even unto your dying days on planet Earth. You may not all become parents but you have all experienced what it was like to be a child. This may seem unnecessarily obvious, and yet many people forget it when they become parents themselves. It seems almost as if it is easier to remember the patterns of your parents' child rearing practices than what it was like to be a young child in a family.

Children start out on your physical plane with some considerable advantages as well as a range of disadvantages.

They have the advantage of being far closer to the direct experience of the spiritual realms than the enormous majority of adults. Unless a small child has received considerable anti-spiritual indoctrination whilst in the womb, he or she will be born with a close connection to Me and the spiritual world as a whole. It is during the first few years of life, when at their most vulnerable, that children are at grave risk of having those connections severed by the attitudes of the adults around them. This is a far greater risk in the societies of the "developed world", with their long traditions of theistic religions, than in those societies of the "primitive world" where communities often have a close spiritual connection to the land and all life thereon. Such risks highlight the major disadvantage children are born with, their immense vulnerability.

Another advantage is their ability to experience the world around them relatively unfettered by the assumptions and prejudices that many of you are lumbered with as adults. Given just a little encouragement, children can hold on to this innocent contact with the world for quite some time; it is only the socialisation and schooling processes that destroy it.

Similarly, children have access to immense creativity and imagination in their unschooled state. It takes little encouragement to get the spirit, heart and mind of a human child busily imagining the most creative of games and activities, inventing wondrous things and experiences. And, once again, a real disadvantage of being so young and innocent is the ease with which young children internalise the criticism of adults, which can destroy the spark of creativity each of them brings into the world.

The bulk of the assumptions you make about the need for the heavy socialisation of children stems from a belief that people are born sinful and need to be saved. In reality, the opposite is true: you are all conceived in the image of Me and bring with you into the world your true connection to the Divine. If children were encouraged to develop and maintain that connection rather than having it ridiculed, denied and even beaten out of them, then the whole world would soon become a very different place, not needing to be saved at all.

Let us consider a few general questions on having children.

I know some people worry about the ideal age gap between siblings in families. The answer to such a question will always lie partly within the particular family and the society within which it exists. If the family exists to produce as many children as possible to provide a good chance of some surviving into adulthood and so caring for the parents in their old age, then the issue of how close together children are conceived will tend to be an irrelevance.

If the family exists to provide a loving, safe and supportive environment in which a human being can grow towards fulfilling their human and spiritual potential in this chosen life, then closeness in age is a definite issue. In an ideal environment, every child could do with the full attention of the adults in the family to care for them, love them, help them to grow, draw out their potential and find their path to being and expressing who they really are. During the first three to four years, the level of attention required is at its highest, and the emotional threat from a younger sibling arriving on the scene is greatest. The age will vary somewhat from child to child, and can be assessed by the level of security and self-esteem the child displays rather than by the number of years and months they have been out of their mother's womb.

If you chose to live in a world where the enormous abundance that exists in the universe was shared around so that no-one went without, then the social pattern of conceiving children out of fear of the future rather than love of life would no longer exist.

Some of you say that there are risks associated with having only one child in a family. Any such risk is likely to be related to the attitudes and emotional makeup of the parents rather than the child. If a couple are desperate to have more than one child and cannot, that will inevitably affect the one child they have. If they choose to have only one child for reasons that are less than completely sound, such as restricting the degree of disruption to their own lives, once again they are likely to run into problems. The same applies in those few societies where for reasons of population control, harsh measures have been introduced to prevent couples having more than one child.

If you lived in tribes or greatly extended family groups, this issue of the only child would cease to exist. In isolated nuclear family units, with parents who are unaware of the emotional, spiritual and social issues entailed in guiding children through their early years, bringing up an only child can be quite problematic for all concerned. The greatest risk is that unaware parents may encourage thoughts, beliefs, attitudes and behaviour in their child based on their own unresolved childhood experiences and resultant emotional hang-ups. Parents lacking in a high level of personal psychological awareness are at risk of becoming as emotionally dependent on their only child as the child becomes on them, and both sides can become locked in a co-dependent relationship that is not useful for either.

Fully aware and functional parents, on the other hand, who choose to have only one child, will not necessarily experience any of these problems.

Is it perhaps appropriate for some people to decide against having children at all? It would serve you well to be more consciously aware of your motivation for bringing children into the world. Many people do it without thinking about it. They may do it because it is expected of them, or because it is just such an easy part of the physical process of being a sexually active human being. Even those who consciously set out to conceive a child do not necessarily take great trouble to examine whether their reasons for wanting to do so really reflect both their own spiritual journey and that of the being they will be bringing into the world.

There was a time when the decision to have children was never an issue. That was before there came to be almost six billion of you on the planet. Now, it seems absurd that such a significant decision, for you personally as well as for the species as a whole, is not taken with a whole lot more awareness than it is.

There are two questions that need to be asked: Is becoming a parent a full reflection of who you really are in the universe? Is having a child a humanly responsible thing to do for the planet and its inhabitants?

The time is rapidly approaching when you will shift the basis of family life on the planet. A move towards a more tribal way of being in the world would remove some of the current reasons for having children. It would provide a far more viable support structure for parents and children, so making the task easier and more fulfilling for all concerned. It would also do away with the need for all adults to become parents as the only way to have a loving relationship with children, and so experiencing one of the great joys of human life.

Until such changes start to take place, it is wholly appropriate for an increasing number of people actively to decide not to bring children into the world at all.

I know that in some parts of the world, people are

beginning to question whether perhaps society should make such decisions for parents.

It is difficult to change the social patterns laid down over generations. However, it is questionable whether that is a reason for society to take decisions on child-bearing away from couples. In an ideal world, the role of the community and the extended family would be to help couples decide whether it was appropriate for them to have children. Society's role in this process would best be as educator and provider of the information necessary to allow people to reach their own decisions.

It is also true that the hugely rapid increase in population over a short period of time has made it extremely hard for your societies to bring about the cultural shifts required for change. As such, you may all have to accept that there is a social role in ensuring population control. It may be preferable to accept this, rather than to face the natural consequences of over-populating your planet.

7. Raising Children or Guiding them through Life

You have something of a problem with your use of language in the context of growing children. So many of the phrases you use suggest passivity on the part of the child and active control on the part of the adults concerned. And herein are contained some of the problems that you face.

There is no doubt that children and young people need assistance and guidance to survive and grow effectively on the spiritual, emotional, physical and intellectual levels. They need to learn about what works and what doesn't in their attitudes to and behaviour in the world they inhabit. They need to discover, without too much personal cost, the ways of their families and societies in order to know how to live social lives.

At the same time, they need to be helped to understand and appreciate their individuality, their freedom and their responsibilities, without undue pressure to conform to some arbitrary code of social conduct that may be at odds with the possibility of realising their soul purpose. To succeed in living towards their universal life purpose, they need to be able to know what it means to be a spiritual being having a human experience. They need to be able to stretch their spiritual, emotional and intellectual as well as physical muscles in all sorts of ways. They need every opportunity to come to understand that they have choice about how to be and what to do in this life, free from the value-based judgments and admonitions of the adult world.

As parents, you have the task of finding an effective balance between allowing children to grow freely with awareness, and helping them to understand the constraints of the social world in which you all live. This is most hard in the technological, consumerist countries where your lifestyle is so much at odds with a balanced spiritual way of being. It is easiest amongst the few remaining indigenous peoples of your world who live close to nature, as part of a holistic system which has a balanced regard for the sacred and the profane.

Terms like "raising children", "rearing them", "bringing them up" all speak of too much adult control over the process. To think rather of guiding them through the adventure that is life brings an appropriate element of mystery that better suits the task of learning how to be human.

Parents are regularly blamed for not adequately socialising their children. The anti-social behaviour of young people on the streets and in schools is seen by many as the result of poor parenting. How do we find a way to marry the demands of society and what You are telling us of the spiritual needs of the child?

In the true course of events these would be one and the same. It is only because your societies have moved away from the spiritual that there is an apparent conflict here. Nevertheless, it is not appropriate to wait until someone has managed to change the society in which you live before you change the way in which you guide children through their growing up. On the contrary, changing patterns of parenting will have a profound impact on the state of society.

The needs of the child and the needs of society are not that different. Both needs would be addressed by a substantial increase in the amount of unconditional love in the world and a corresponding decrease in the amount of fear. Children and young people need a very high level of love and acceptance. They need to be seen for who they really are, spiritual beings coming to terms with a human existence very different from and much more limited than that they are used to in the realms of spirit. They need to be recognised as one with all of life, as part of all life. Each child is in actuality a part of every adult living on the planet today, just as you are all part of each other and every other living thing in the universe. Seen from this perspective, children would benefit from being treated as the shared responsibility of every adult in society, not just their biological parents. As in highly evolved cultures in other parts of the universe, children can be cared for, nurtured and educated by any and every adult around them, growing in a community of spiritual commitment to life itself.

The reason why the lives of children and young people seem to be at odds with maintaining a stable community atmosphere has to do both with the not so effective nature of your communities, and with the way in which children are reared to be largely out of touch with their soul purpose.

In most of the industrialised countries of the world you have created child-unfriendly communities and societies in the name of progress and development. Your lives run at a pace that is too fast for little people; your world has become too full of dangerous technology, which poses a threat to their very survival. Your demand for consumerist production has taken people out of the communities into factories, depriving children of the very adults they need around them to learn from. Your increasing pattern of shifting scale ever upwards has meant continued centralisation, depriving local communities of facilities and amenities that might otherwise help to compensate for the absence of the extended family, and your perceived need for a compliant, literate workforce has established long hours of schooling frequently at odds with the emotional and spiritual development of children. We will talk more about this in Chapter Nine on Education and Schooling.

You have grown too quickly. The pace of technological development has far outstripped your ability to manage the social and environmental consequences of such rapid change. And children, young people and families are taking the brunt of the pain all this is creating.

What can we begin to do positively about shifting from child rearing to guiding our children's growth, given the state of society around us?

The only way you are going to bring about a change in the way you guide children through life is to shift the way you live in your local communities. And the only way you are going to bring about long-term permanent shifts in the way you live is to change your ways of being and doing with children.

Faced with a description of all the things that are not working, the idea of change may feel quite daunting, but with My help and that of others in the world who love you, much will be achieved. Start with yourself. Start by making a conscious decision to choose love rather than fear in every minute of your day. Whenever you react negatively, out of fear about what others will think of you, or what your internalised parental voice tells you is right or wrong, remember to love yourself and give yourself credit for doing the best you know how, given your background and your past experience and any training you have received. Turn the fear of judgment into a love of your willingness to be more open and aware of who you really are. Direct the energy that goes into your struggle to get it right into choosing to become more aware of yourself and others as spiritual creatures in a human world. Open yourself to the help that is to be found all around you. You are surrounded by the glory of life on earth, the wisdom of nature and a myriad spiritual energies waiting patiently in the wings for the awakening of the spirit in humankind. Remember that I am always present and willing to help you in your life journey.

As you start to work on your own spiritual and emotional awakening you will inevitably start to see and experience your children differently. Be aware of them as young beings born to experience life in the physical so that they can come to discover who they really are. Love them and help them, as they struggle to fit into an adult world that is far from user-friendly. Remember what it was like to be a child yourself, and offer them guidance in finding their connection to the spiritual side of life from which they can draw unlimited support to help them with the human side.

Above all, avoid instilling fear in them as it probably was instilled in you as a child. It is such a common pattern to use threats and warnings of dire consequences as a way of controlling children's behaviour – "If you don't wear your seat belt the policeman will lock you up"; "If you don't eat your vegetables, you won't grow"; "If you don't do your homework, you'll not get on at school." Such common attempts to control children surround them with fear energy rather than love energy. They come to accept this as the norm, and live their lives in the expectation of fear. They learn to be fearful of situations and people, and act from a fear base to others in their turn.

It seems to be easier and quicker to use threats and promises to impose control. In the short term it is, but operating from this short-term view is an example of the damage done by not taking into account the bigger picture of life. Like the use of violence that "did me no harm as a child", it perpetuates detrimental patterns of behaviour, making it harder for you to achieve your soul purpose.

Find ways to communicate with love for your children as much of the time as possible. Appeal to the love in them, for themselves and for you and other people. Help them to learn that it is love that enhances life, while fear limits it. That is the single most important thing you can do both for your children and for the world as a whole.

All young people need your help and guidance about how to be in the world. And they need guidance about how to learn rather than simple rote learning. Find a way to learn alongside them, rather than starting from the false belief that you already have all the answers to pass down to them.

Remember that unconditional love does not entail a lack of boundaries nor a permissive approach to parenting that allows children to run riot and cause harm to themselves or other people. The mountain guide will refuse to take a climber on routes that are too dangerous. He or she will provide clear instructions for handling specific situations as they come up which are best not learnt through disastrous mistakes. "No" is such a crucially important word that it should be used seldom and then with great wisdom, lest its value gets lost in daily repetition. Put your emphasis on encouraging ways of being and doing that stem from love rather than fear. Avoid getting yourself and your children into patterns and situations where they have to be discouraged, and when you can't, find ways that still emphasise love rather than fear.

For yourselves, recognise the limitations of living in nuclear families isolated from other families. You can choose many ways of starting to break down the barriers between you and other people. If you really want to make a difference to your lives and those of your children, explore opportunities now coming on to the scene for different styles of living, such as the building of intentional communities[3]. You are not the only people likely to be feeling isolated; there are probably others in your street who are also fearful and depressed about the struggle of life. Open up the barriers between you, reach out with love and find others whom you can relate to, with whom you can spend time and share your spiritual journey, and begin to rebuild a sense of community around you.

Having small children opens many doors. If you operate from an attitude of marvelling at the beauty of life around you and take on some of the sheer inquisitiveness of your children, you will find it easy to discover other parents also looking for a different way of being and doing in the world.

Life is a journey, not a prison sentence. Encourage your children to journey as far and wide as possible on all planes of existence. Encourage them to stretch their imaginations, to open up their hearts, to develop the spiritual awareness and connections they were born with, as well as flexing their muscles and honing their bodies. Share in their adventure, following their lead while monitoring their safety. Help to protect them from the many less than useful aspects of life in your western societies. Substitute walks in the park or the woods for hours in front of the television, free-form painting for comics and video games, storytelling for learning to read.

This is admirably idealistic, yet many of us live frenetic lives trying to cope with earning a living and rely upon television and video games to baby-sit our children. I don't want to feel guilty doing so.

I do not ask that you strive to do these things out of some moral need to get it right. I ask that you accept the unlimited unconditional love that I have to offer which will support you to make the little changes in your lives and your parenting that can make a difference in the world. It is easy to feel daunted. Every journey begins with just a few steps in the right direction; the most important step is to make the commitment to start out, even before you believe that you have what it takes to complete it. I will not only accompany you on the journey, but will also willingly carry you at times when the going gets really tough.

Sometimes it requires little more than questioning the content and process of every activity you introduce your children to. Ask yourselves: "How far is this a model of love or of fear?"; "To what extent does this challenge imagination and creativity, or just present ready-made ideas?" and "Am I just pushing them too hard to succeed?"

The human child takes a lot longer than most people realise to fully join the adult world. Using the intellect is very much a part of the adult world, which should be left until the child has reached a stage of development suited to it. For most children this is some time between seven and twelve years of age. Until that time, the use of the mind to be encouraged is in the area of imagination and creativity, understanding patterns and form, colour and shapes, rather than rational understanding. Early childhood development requires a good holistic mix of activities without too much emphasis on external stimulation. Help your young children to develop their awareness and understanding of life on the levels of heart, spirit, mind and body, playing and testing out their abilities and talents in as free and unstructured a way as possible.

There is plenty of time for intellectual and technical learning. The desire to push children into formal education so young most often stems from fear, not love. It stems from parents' fear that their children will be disadvantaged in the educational system if they don't have a good start. It stems from your society's fear that inadequate socialisation is the root cause of the social unrest you are increasingly experiencing. Neither of these fears is justified.

Children with a narrow intellectual focus will usually fare least well in journeying towards the fulfilment of their soul purpose. And the root cause of your immense social problems is the separation of humanity from Me, with the resulting prevalence of fear. You would do your children and your global society a far better service if you encouraged them to develop their understanding of themselves, their appreciation of nature and the planet on which they grow, so maintaining and enhancing their innate connection to Me and all things spiritual. Help them to develop their ability to love themselves and others, to see fear as an aberration rather than the norm, and to celebrate the Divine in all things. Educate the senses, the heart and the body, and allow the education of the intellect to follow on naturally through a holistic process of maturing into adulthood.

If my children are not getting such a rounded education in school, what can I do as a parent to provide it at home?

Take a moment to review the activities your child and you as a family engage in over a day or a week. List the different ways in which all the human senses are being stimulated and educated through these activities. What is the interplay between their experience of colour and pattern, shape and form, between tone and timbre, volume and pitch? How do they experience texture, shape and form with their hands? How open are you to intuition and spiritual stimuli? When you have reviewed the current state of play, plan simple ways to make up for any imbalance: introduce more music making, more painting and drawing, more modelling with modelling clay or play dough, more expeditions to discover insects under the bark of trees, more visits to the next-door neighbour to play with the new kittens. Follow your child's interest.

There are many resource books[4] available that can introduce you to creative play and education with young children, offering guidance on indoor and outdoor activities. You do not have to be knowledgeable about art, music or creative play, so long as you are open to the adventure of learning and enjoying life to the full alongside your children.

8. Nature versus Nurture

Seen from a spiritual perspective, this subject raises almost no debate. The issue is not so much whether a child is born a certain way or created that way by those who nurture him or her. What more usefully can be discussed here are the workings of choice and its connection to what some people refer to as karma.

The incarnating soul can and often does choose to bring into its new life on earth elements carried over from previous physical lives. This is in order to provide the opportunity for continued learning in the greater fulfilment of soul purpose. Contrary to popular belief, it is not some form of punishment for wrongs committed in a past life nor a reward for good service. The natural law of the Universe lays down life in its widest sense, that is physical and spiritual, as being about regaining the awareness of your godliness and healing the felt separation from Me. Each new physical life you choose to take on provides you with opportunities for growing and learning in this great adventure in Universal Existence. You get to choose the parts you play, and you may well choose to set up specific aspects of them prior to incarnating. On some level, when such elements are connected to the "type" of character you choose to be born as, we might say that aspects of your "nature" are fixed prior to conception.

Even when this is the case, you have freedom to choose your parents and the sort of environment into which you are born. You also each have freedom of choice over how you live the lives you choose. The vast majority of you find it very hard to realise and act on that freedom. In **On Life**, and in the Introduction to this book, we talked about the three ways in which you create your own reality through the power of thought.

You create the world around you, and your experience in it and of it, through the unconscious thoughts you take on board during the most impressionable years of your early childhood. In this sense, the style and degree of your nurturing as a child has a profound impact on your development as a human being.

You can also create your experience of life and the world around you through contributing to and colluding with the unconscious collective thoughts of the society or community in which you live. This can also to some extent be seen as an element of the effect of nurture rather than nature.

The third, and unfortunately least common, way to generate the world around you and your experience of it, is through the conscious application of aware thought. The majority of children do not develop their full power in this respect before they have become hugely influenced by the other two. Child rearing practices in most parts of the world are fixed on aiming to ensure that the combination of parental, familial and social pressure on the individual's way of thinking is so great that the individual's control over their own reality is often impossible to affect consciously.

It is for this reason that nurture has such a profound impact on the life of the child as it grows into adulthood. This is why many people do not manage to establish enough spiritual consciousness to live out the path their soul laid down for them in this life.

I would suggest to you from My observations that of the two, nurture plays a far larger part than nature. And that it would be more useful if it were otherwise.

It is indeed strange that in the English language you choose these two words to discuss this issue. What you do for your children is not particularly nurturing, and what they bring with them into the world has far more to do with spirit than with nature.

If you were truly nurturing of children on a holistic level, then the act of guiding them through their growing up, and encouraging them to develop their spirits and hearts as well as minds and bodies, would allow them more opportunity to make conscious choices about their lives and live out their true "nature" more fully.

Can You please suggest some specific ways in which we could decrease the effect of "nurture" and increase that of "nature"?

It is too easy for you to adopt expectations for your offspring, to project into their lives all the things you might have wanted to have or to be when you were little. Start by realising that you will always be at risk of trying to re-live your own childhood through your children. This is a fact of human life in its normal rather unaware state, and not something to beat yourself up about. Recognise the risk, and know that by avoiding it you actually stand a greater chance of healing your own childhood hurts while guiding your children.

Be open to seeing your children for who they really are at a soul level, rather than who you want them to become. Allow them the freedom to explore their identity within the bounds of safety and the widest limits to socially acceptable behaviour you feel confident to impose. Let them grow at their own rate; do not push them to grow faster because that is what everyone else is doing, nor hold them back for fear that they will outgrow their peers. Develop for yourself an understanding of child development that includes a full awareness of the emotional and the spiritual as well as the physical and intellectual, and then recognise that rates of development differ hugely from one child to the next. Beware any theories of child development that do not include a spiritual framework, since they are thus disregarding a critical ingredient of the first ten years of life.

Ask yourself at every turn whose need is being met by any new decision to encourage or dissuade your children on a particular path. "Am I doing this out of love because it really represents an accurate balance between the child's needs and our family/society's needs?" "Am I allowing the spiritual nature of my child to shine through, even as I help them to learn the importance of social living?" If the answer to either question is no, be willing to let go of the fear that often drives parents to start socialising their young too soon, too heavy-handedly or simply inappropriately.

9. Education and Schooling

From the universal perspective, education and schooling are an extension of the subject of raising versus guiding children. Schooling falls into the raising camp whilst education falls into that of guiding. There is a place for both as children, young people and indeed adults go about their task of growing and maturing in your world.

Let us talk first about education. As many of you already know, education is a life-long process that starts in the womb and ends in this life as you breathe your last human breath and pass back to the realm of spirit. Education isn't something you do to some people and not others, something some people receive and others miss out on. It is happening all around you all the time. Every move a baby makes, every experience a child has, every thought that goes through a teenager's head has an educative effect. Education is something you experience continually in every area of life. In this sense of the word, education is a reactive response to life, a way of learning by reaction to what goes on around you and indeed largely by re-activating what you already know.

There are also many things that it will be useful to know about that you will not discover solely by living life to the full and reacting to what happens around you: history, philosophy and the inner workings of the human psyche, to name a few. Such subject matter requires a proactive process of discovery and education, a reaching out for new understanding, new awareness, knowledge and skill.

Whether you are learning by daily experience or actively seeking out new knowledge, you will usually find it easier and more beneficial if you are helped and guided by someone a step or two further along the road. Effective guides, operating with love and compassion, can add enormously to the value of the educational experience.

In highly evolved societies the role of guide is given to the elders in the community rather than to "professional teachers" who often struggle to provide the guidance needed by large groups of children forced to be in their care for long periods of time. There is little about being locked up in a so-called educational establishment that is conducive to education. Most of you know this in your hearts, yet readily ignore it in your heads.

To promote the education of the young in your care and control, you would be wise to start taking a much more holistic approach. The human being goes through certain developmental stages in growing from a new-born physical incarnation of a spiritual life form to a fully-grown specimen of manhood or womanhood. A fundamental mistake you have come to make in your schooling process is to ignore these developmental stages and force children to tackle educational tasks they are not ready for.

During the first years of a child's life he or she is still very close to the spiritual realms. Children need help to become comfortable with the physical reality they experience in a way that recognises their continued connection to the Divine and the realms of spirit. Learning to be in the body, and to experience the full range of human emotions, is the task of the child in the first seven to twelve years of life. If they can be helped to do this at the same time as grounding their spirituality on this planet, they will develop a solid connection with life on earth.

Allow them to experiment with their physicality and their emotions long before you start introducing them to the world of the intellect. Help them to maintain their acceptance and understanding of the spiritual through connection with the natural world, through ritual and through an acceptance of their own spiritual experience, which is often discounted by parents as pure imagination.

You have time-honoured ways of helping children to appreciate the world around them and develop a simple understanding of life that requires little intellectual analysis. Storytelling is perhaps the most universal way, whilst the playing of games that tap into the imagination and allow children to work things through in their own minds can be very beneficial.

Children have no need to learn to read or write, to use computers or other machines or understand the technical world of the adult until they are ready to join that world. Such readiness does not come until they have developed their full physicality and learnt to live fully in the complete range of human emotions. On some level, such readiness never comes if these two tasks are not also completed with full conscious awareness of their spirituality. For most children, this transition from incarnating child to small adult is not complete until somewhere between the ages of nine and twelve. Each child will take his or her own time and no child can be forced.

Be wary of over-filling the early years with stimulation and distraction. Small children need very little to keep them focused on learning, exploring and experimenting. They do not need to be surrounded by complicated action toys, games, puzzles, and activities better suited to the next stage in their development. Activities and toys that detract from the child's ability to use his or her own imagination are particularly damaging to the natural development of a whole, healthy child. It makes no sense to Me to see so many of you sitting your children in front of television for hours on end, and supplying them with video games and toys that only deprive them of their creativity and instil in them adult values – which are themselves highly suspect in their lack of potential to help them fulfil their soul purpose in life.

If you could appreciate the damage this approach does to the hearts and souls, not to mention the minds, of your current generation of children, you would choose to stop doing it now.

Children would be much better off spending time out of doors, digging in the soil, playing with colours and shapes, animals and plants, angels and fairies, stretching their imagination and creativity, listening with wonder to stories and learning to invent their own. And it is best if this is all done under the watchful eye of mature and wise people who will shower them with unconditional love and slowly and gently guide them in their activities and behaviour without trying to force them into moulds.

Let us now turn to the subject of schooling. By this term I mean passing on to someone a particular set of behaviours or skills that will be of value to them in the life they are to lead. You school an adult in how to drive a car; you school a young person in the fundamentals of using a computer. Both these activities require an element of technical knowledge which has to be learnt before the individual can go on to fully educate themselves in the use of the car or the computer.

From this perspective, schooling is akin to instruction or training and separate from the process of education. I would advocate the use of the term schooling for children in much the same way as you use it with animals. You school a horse to walk, run and jump in a particular style. There are some practical aspects of a child's life that you also can usefully school them in.

The confusion occurs because you have developed a system of schooling which you consider to be education, when little of it really is. It is not a mistake that the places where parents send their children to be educated are called schools. My observation is that across most of your planet, attendance at school is for the purpose of instruction and socialisation, whereas education is left largely to chance.

It would be possible to do away with schools completely. Most highly evolved societies on your planet do not segregate their children away in schools, and amongst the highly evolved beings of the universe the concept is completely unknown. There is nothing that has to be taught that cannot be undertaken as part of a wider process of growing, learning, and living life to the full.

Schools have become so important in the world partly because you find it too easy to see only parts of a system at a time, and then respond to what you see with fear and distrust rather than love and trust. You believe you see a need to teach children the rudiments of social behaviour, intellectual understanding and how to communicate on paper, and you see these things in virtual isolation from the spiritual, emotional and social nature of life on the planet. You then react to the need you believe you see in a controlling and deterministic way that is both driven by fear and engenders fear in those involved.

Your determination to school children throughout the

world has in the past been driven by the fear that an un-schooled workforce will not be able to satisfy the demands of growth. Added to this now is the fear that an un-schooled mass in the world poses a potential threat to the social and economic order you have created. Without socialisation in the ways of consuming and developing, the unschooled masses could shift from ineffectively contributing to your global race for growth to becoming a positive force for resistance and so a threat to that global race.

Of course each individual parent willingly sending their child to school believes that they are doing so for the good of the child's future. Just as each individual teacher in those schools sees him- or herself not as an organ of socialisation and control so much as a saviour from illiteracy and ignorance. Yet some of the most illiterate and "ignorant" people in the world are those closest to Me, most connected to the world in which they live and by far happier, more loving and less fearful than any of you in the "civilised" world today.

Yet all is not lost. I observe schooling as not working in the universal order of things on planet Earth. Its dysfunction is precisely what provides you now with the opportunity to work towards education in a holistic form. That in turn could help you all to progress in achieving your soul purposes.

It will take a lot to convince you all to do away with schools as you know them. There are intermediate stages in that process, one of which those involved in home education have been advocating provocatively for years. If you made schools voluntary rather than compulsory, then they would have to offer a form of education that would excite children and entice them in, rather than providing them with schooling that is largely irrelevant to life and fails to hold their attention.

Do not underestimate the power of the popular vote. If you all start to operate with love rather than fear, abandoning the fear that your children will miss out by not going to school, and if you decide to keep them at home in their millions, the school system would change quite rapidly!

Under ideal conditions, schools would be unnecessary because children would learn alongside the significant adults in their families, tribes and communities. They would learn by apprenticeship and through the gentle loving guidance of all the people and all the non-human life forms in their local environment.

In practice, it would be possible to develop ways of gathering children together in institutions that would greatly reduce the damage done in current nurseries and schools. There are attempts to do this going on around you all the time; the worldwide movement of Steiner Waldorf[5] Kindergartens and Schools comes about the closest to avoiding many of the damaging aspects of conventional schooling, even though it could do with evolving in the light of present needs rather than holding on to traditional practices.

What is needed are changes to current approaches:

You could do with a far greater number of adults available to guide children through their daily learning activities. Instead of class ratios of one to thirty or more, you would be wise to have ratios more like one to three or four. As already stated, teachers would better be chosen for their maturity and wisdom than their technical or intellectual competence.

In the first seven or eight years, avoid teaching any intellectually demanding subjects. The three "R"s could be valuably removed from the curriculum altogether, and replaced by painting, music, creative play, caring for animals and plants, and learning reverence for all things natural and each other.

Allow a free expression of the human heart and spirit, so that small children can learn who and what they are as well as how to behave in the world.

Avoid forcing them into competitive ways of behaving, and respect their natural inclination for individuality and possessiveness. Children forced to share before they are ready can experience all sorts of emotional problems.

Concentrate on helping them to learn ways of being together with other children and adults that are co-operative and loving rather than fearful and antagonistic, whilst still always being willing to allow the free expression even of feelings that may appear to be negative in the moment.

Do as much as possible to make a connection between home and school. If it is not possible for parents and grandparents to guide children through their early years of education at home, then educational institutions should at least ensure that there is as small a gap as possible be-tween the home experience and that at school.

You are talking here about a real revolution in our edu-cational system.

Let Me repeat what I said in My introduction. Throughout the **God Speaks** collection I am proposing a real revolution in the way you lead your lives. If you wish to ensure that you can continue to live on planet Earth for the foreseeable future, then revolution is what is needed now before it is too late. What is needed is a decision by thou-sands of millions of people throughout your planet that enough is enough, that the time has come to be the mas-ters and mistresses of your own spiritual destiny.

10. Co-operation versus Competition

One of the universal truths we discussed at some length in our first book was that all living things in the universe are part of one whole that is Me. You and every person you might wish to compete with are part of the same living entity. On a spiritual level you are all one. Does it make any sense at all to compete with parts of you?

Competition keeps you firmly stuck in your spiritual evolution. It would be useful for you to decide whether a competitive social order satisfies the fundamental purpose of human life: to explore, define and express who you really are on a spiritual level. It is my desire that you decide in favour of co-operation and against competition. So let us consider the possibilities offered by co-operation before we look at the ways in which competition does you no favours.

You live on an abundant planet in an abundant universe. You are surrounded by the beauty and riches of nature. You bask in the light of the Holy Spirit, the life force that flows through and connects every element of the universe. The potential for joy and glory in your lives is limitless. Naturally, so is the potential for you to turn away from Me and live in the shadow of fear that exists side by side with My love.

I gave you freedom of choice and expect you to take responsibility for how you use it. I also gave you the power to create the world around you. You do this in three steps: you think, you speak and you act that which you desire to create. As we have said elsewhere, there are three ways you think your reality into existence: through your unconscious thoughts, through the unconscious thoughts of the groups you are a part and through your own conscious thought processes.

I created the Universe in order to have the experience of knowing Myself as I really am. To do that, I chose to create life and set it – you – the task to come to know who you really are, so that, ultimately you can return to being One with Me. As I explained in **On Life** this required life as you know it to experience itself as separate from Me, otherwise we would not be able to have the experience of knowing the other and so knowing the self.

In your great adventure to come to know yourselves and so come to know and re-member yourselves with Me, I gave you the power of total unconditional love. Love is the energy that powers life in the universe. And, by the same token of opposites, I created love's shadow – fear.

These are the fundamental spiritual principles that govern your lives and My universe. Put them together and I trust that you can begin to see why co-operation makes sense.

If you work together you can align the three aspects of creative thought and so increase exponentially your ability to generate the world you wish to live in. If you work together you will move towards making the same choices in life. If you choose to work together you will start to take full responsibility not only for yourselves but also for all life on planet Earth and eventually beyond it. If you work together you can ensure that the abundance of your home planet is maintained for the benefit of all life that inhabits it. If you work together you can speed up the process of human spiritual evolution and so move more firmly towards healing your separation from Me.

In co-operation you can enhance your individual power to levels you can currently only dream of. There will be no limit to what humanity can achieve on earth. You can fulfil your destiny as guardians of the physical realms you enjoy. You can create the heaven on earth that you have aspired to for generations. Working together, all is possible.

And in time you will not be limited to planet Earth. Working in co-operation, you will be able to extend your experience outwards to the stars. With you co-operating, there will be no reason for the rest of the universe to be concerned about your attempts to reach the stars. You will be welcomed with open arms by your brothers and sisters in your galaxy.

Even now, acting in co-operation you have the ability to eradicate poverty and ill health from your world. Working together you could immediately begin to heal your environment and set the planet back on course to a secure future. Working alongside each other with love rather than fear you could heal the rifts between peoples and countries, turn swords into ploughshares and make communities whole again.

All of this and more is open to you when you all choose co-operation over competition.

And yet, right now competition is part of the very makeup of your social and economic structures. This stems from your adopted fear that there will never be enough to go round – not enough power, influence, friendship, work, cash, status, food, possessions or anything else. Which is of course factually incorrect. The universe is an abundant place. Even planet Earth could continue to sustain life for millions of years with no risk to itself or any element of that life, if you avoid making growth and technology more important that humanity and spirituality.

There is nothing achieved through the expression of fear in competition that could not be more easily and more fruitfully achieved through the expression of love in co-operation. Together you will always be able to do more, generate more and produce more than you can when you are split up into factions and warring tribes, whether as nations or local businesses.

If competition is such a negative element of our human-ness, how come it has been around for such a long time?

I am not sure it is valid to say that it is a "negative element of your humanness". For a start it isn't part of being human so much as part of being social humans. Among the traditional peoples of your planet, there have been tribes who did not compete for the important things in life, either within their own tribes or between tribes. The tribal peoples who developed into war-like societies chose the road of fear rather than love and interdependence at some early point in their social development; it was not innate in their makeup.

Competition is far more of a male characteristic than female and seems particularly to flourish wherever high levels of schooling take place. This should suggest to you that competition is a learnt response to fear-based teaching rather than an innate characteristic of your humanity.

Look at competition in the light of how you actually live on the planet. Everything you all need exists in abundance. The relatively rare things for which you end up competing are those that you want but do not really need. Under normal earthly conditions there is enough air, water and land to go round. All the basic raw materials you have needed in the past have always existed in copious quantities. It is only in the last sixty years or so that you have started "needing" metals such as uranium that are hard to come by. Most of the expensive things in life you do not need. You can operate in the world without anything precious.

Competition started to arise on the planet when you shifted from a mentality of stewardship into one of ownership. Once you operate from a mentality that says "I can own something and so keep it from someone else", you start to establish unreal values for the rarer commodities. Along with the fear of loss that is established through ownership there comes the need to acquire more than others, and so competition is born. We discussed elements of this thinking in the chapter on money in **On Life**. You do not need to compete for what belongs to everyone. In reality, everything belongs to everyone and so competition is unnecessary.

Competition is no longer limited to issues of wealth or possession. It is encouraged in almost every aspect of life. Children are taught to compete with each other all the time, as to who is fastest, ablest, cleverest, funniest, prettiest and more. By the time children go to formal school they have been firmly indoctrinated with the idea of competing. They soon come to understand that in order to succeed someone else has to fail, that to do well inevitably means that someone else does badly. It is hardly surprising that by the time they leave school they are completely at home with the belief that there can be no rich without the poor, no well-fed without the hungry, no safety without the fearful, no healthy without the sick. They have been set on the scramble to compete for everything in their lives and so have well internalised the fear that they were exposed to in your basic child-rearing practices.

Many people make valiant efforts to argue that co-operation is more effective than competition, yet we don't seem to make progress. How come?

You will make progress in lessening competition, just as in education, child-rearing and most other areas, when you address your fundamental practice of opting for fear rather than love. You cannot do away with competition and continue to live in fear. If fear is the emotion you wish to live with, then competition, aggression, violence, disease and social unrest are all part of the equation.

Albert Einstein is quoted as saying that you cannot solve a problem from within the way of thinking that gave rise to it. How do we begin to do away with the fear and so address all these issues when we are so fear-full?

This is where you can usefully remember that you have full freedom of choice. You are fearful, not because you have anything to be afraid of, but because you choose to be full of fear. It would serve you well to shift your thinking from the outside to the inside. Recognise the total degree to which you create the reality in which you live and your experience of the world.

People ask how come two people living in similar circumstances often have such different experiences of life. The answer lies in their thinking and feeling. In the same situation, one person can choose to look at the world through the filter of love and experience love reflected back to them; another can choose the filter of fear and experience only fear reflected back. It starts with you!

So what of the competition that motivates people to do their best, strive for success, push ahead in their lives? What of economic competition that weeds out the inefficient firms and leaves only those best able to supply our needs?

Let us start with how competition motivates people to do their best, to strive for success and push ahead in their lives. Competition does have the effect of pushing ahead those people who feel they have a chance of getting to or near the top. For people who have chosen unconsciously to exist in the middle or towards the bottom, competition does little to encourage or motivate them. On the contrary, it can be constantly demotivating and reinforce feelings of failure, so creating self-fulfilling prophecies.

The more important question to be considered is how much more effective would be a genuine loving atmosphere of co-operation? You have plenty of examples around you of how much more effective good teamwork is than individuals competing with each other. Strip away the fear that pervades your thinking and feeling, and the joy of collaborative achievement, the delight in mutual success and the companionship of doing things well together will have a motivating power far greater than the fear of failure generated by competition.

As to economic competition, I would challenge you all to look at what you need rather than what you want, or what the big companies controlling your economies decide you want. Do you really need mega-supermarkets on out of town sites selling enormous ranges of food and consumer goods more than you need local corner shops and a sense of thriving community? I observe the destruction of local communities in so many countries of your world with some sorrow. You are choosing to box yourselves further and further into an unsustainable corner from which it will become increasingly hard to escape. You are set on breaking down much of the human, social and economic infrastructure that has served you well for centuries and putting monuments to technology in its place.

You may have become convinced that you need one enormous, efficient, computerised store where ten local shops used to suffice. You may believe that you need competition to cut down the costs of food air freighted around the world to provide you with a diet that no longer changes with the seasons and fits the natural rhythm of life. You may believe that the motor car is the salvation of all your personal problems.

Or you may wake up and realise that you don't need any of these things at all. That your needs are few and simple, and it is the satisfaction of your **wants** that is taking you towards the brink of disaster.

We will consider economic competition more fully in later books. Let it be enough for now to say that economic competition, just like individual competition, is born of fear and akin to a cancer in the body of the human race.

You have all been doing the best you can, given the social context in which you have grown up, your life experiences and the understanding you have managed to acquire of yourselves and your world. There is much to be loved and admired in the human race. You have such potential for care, compassion, beauty, creativity and both human and spiritual wisdom. I have made many efforts in the past, and will make many more in the future, to help you open your eyes, your hearts and your minds to the wider glory of My kingdom, so that you can finds ways of living that will provide you and all other living things on planet Earth with a better quality of life.

You will not achieve this through competition with each other, with nature, with other life forms or the planet as a whole. You will achieve it through co-creation with all that I have surrounded you with, and with great love for yourselves and each other.

11. Children, Toys and Violence

One way you can start to make the shift away from competition towards a co-operative way of being is to address the issue of children, toys and violence. Violence stems from fear and so is counter-productive to the power of love. It is necessary for the young of your race to grow up with an understanding of fear and its role in the world. It is also necessary for them to grow up with a healthy respect for violence so that they can avoid it throughout their lives.

Remember that the power of the creative process is such that you attract into your life that which you fear. So it is not useful to engender a fear of violence in young people, lest they attract the very thing into their lives that you wish them to avoid.

What is needed throughout their formative years is a huge amount of love and a minimisation of fear and all the violence that stems from it. The model you can most usefully provide for them includes of all those aspects of the world in which you live that are love-based rather than fear-based. Provide them with toys, games, activities and exercises that depict and enhance the way love operates now, and could operate even more powerfully.

When your children come into contact with games of violence in whatever form and are curious about them, help them to see the ways in which they are fear-based and steer them towards others that are built around love. There are many opportunities for you to develop creativity, co-operation, growth, artistic expression, care for your environment and all living things, that there really is no need for fear-based entertainment or activities.

So why is it so hard for parents to avoid exposing children to violence and aggression or providing them with toys of war and destruction?

Because they have bought into the social reality of your world which says such things are appropriate. Look around you. How many attempts to resolve conflicts peacefully and civilly do you find, compared with the number of newspaper articles and news broadcasts that depict violence? Violence has become an acceptable part of your world and is doing great harm in making you all immune to the lack of love around you.

Unconditional love has become a concept that few understand and even fewer practise daily. It is hard for people to grasp its importance or understand how to break out of the mould of fear and aggression that you have largely given in to. Those who maintain that the depiction of violence on television or through games is harmless have become over-tolerant of the level of fear and pain on your planet. By colluding with it, they effectively encourage it.

There is little real point in speaking out against injustice and violence in the world out there, while encouraging its growth through your children's education and play at home and at school. Each parent can appropriately take personal responsibility for generating love rather than fear in their children's lives. Help your children to understand the world of violence and fear; do all you can to provide models of a love-based way of life, and do your best to avoid the models of fear-based ways of living.

The issue of violence on television and in films raises its head periodically in the press, and there is always a hearty protest from those who make, distribute or otherwise manage programmes and films disclaiming any proven connection between what children watch and violence in their behaviour.

Right now in your world, violence, aggression and fear make more money than does love. This is often used to "prove" that the public wants violence more than any of the alternatives. However, this argument does not stand up against the best-selling movies of all time, which are tales of love and romance, courage and honesty.

The problem is that violence portrayed in your entertainment media is too effective at influencing the attitudes of people throughout society. It has so dulled their sensitivities that they are now very willing to accept more; indeed the more they are fed, the more they want. This feeding of violence to the population is an effective way of maintaining the total levels of fear in the world. And maintaining these levels is a necessary part of maintaining the world as you know it, a world of economic and social order that pits human against human and against all the life and natural resources on the planet. Too many people are making too much money exploiting others and the environment to be able to accept the common sense that is right in front of them.

The only way you will ultimately stop film and television companies providing violent and fearful models for you to emulate, and the toy manufacturers from giving your children the props to act out those models, will be to take personal responsibility in your millions for boycotting them. There are many people for whom the connection is obvious between violent toys, films and programmes and violence on the streets, in the home and around the world. Such people need to heed this wake-up call, start to lovingly educate their families and friends about the damage being caused, and choose to do something different.

What about violence and aggression in children's behaviour? What do we do about the aggression that is already there?

Introduce them to alternative ways of resolving their differences and getting their needs met. If you are unsure how to do this, there are plenty of books, courses and even counsellors who can introduce you to win-win conflict resolution, negotiation skills, the power of love in listening to and understanding each other and getting your needs met[6]. Help your children to understand that love is a more effective way of resolving conflicts than fear. Help them to discover for themselves how much more they get out of play with their friends and life generally when they are loving, accepting and co-operative than when they are fearful and aggressive.

This might take time, and above all modelling. In all things, parents act as the most powerful models for their children, who in turn model their behaviour on their parents' behaviour. You will not always know the most appropriate ways to behave. When in doubt, ask yourself the question "what is the most loving thing to do now?" Sometimes it will be no more than to tell your children that you want to find a more loving way to behave and need their help. Together you can explore how to be different in the world.

12. Emotions and Children

Let us briefly recap the important points covered in our first book. We wrote that the emotions are perhaps the single most important element of life for you to explore. We said that without a thorough understanding of and acquaintance with the emotions, it is not possible to live life to the full.

The fundamental emotion of the universe is Love. Love is the energy that flows from Me into all life. It is the life force of the universe, the prime energy of creation. We are talking about unconditional love, the energetic positive regard, care and compassion that goes much deeper and wider than the romantic notions of love you tend to restrict the meaning of the word to.

Contrary to popular understanding, the opposite of love is Fear, not hatred. Fear is present whenever love is absent. The fundamental choice you each get to make every moment of the day is whether to feel love or fear. Anything and everything else stems from this.

Love and fear are the energy building blocks of the universe. They exist in all cultures, on all planets, in all physical and spiritual realms. Other emotions have coalesced out of the energy field of the universe in specific areas. Here on Earth, you humans experience three other principal emotions: anger, grief and envy.

Out of these five you develop your full range of emotional experience. Focusing on these will help you to understand and build an awareness of your emotional existence and so increase your moment-by-moment choices in life.

What about shame? Children are often shamed into behaving as adults want them to.

Shame is a behaviour pattern rather than a true emotion; the emotion that goes with it is fear. Shame is a powerful socialising tool that you use widely, not just in families. Through shaming someone you instil such an intense level of fear – fear of rejection, abandonment and even death – that they are willing to adapt their behaviour to better fit your demands. As a result of its widespread use in raising children, the fear associated with shame affects many adults today, restricting their levels of self-esteem as well as their creativity.

The family is the seedbed of emotional life. You learnt what you know and don't know, what you do and don't do, entirely from your own parents, and as parents yourselves you teach your children in like manner. Unless you have done the considerable work of shifting your level of awareness and the emotional patterns built up in the first few years of life, you are likely to pass on to your offspring the same attitudes, values and emotional behaviour that were passed on to you. For this reason alone, education in "emotional intelligence" as Daniel Goleman[7] calls it in his book of that title, is incredibly valuable.

In the womb, a growing child is as near to the purely spiritual state as it is ever likely to be. In this state, before it leaves the safety and security of its mother's body, it can experience only the two universal emotions, love and fear. The three human emotions of anger, grief and envy are overlaid on top of this base during the first few years of life. This is why the emotional state of a newborn baby appears so much simpler than that of a toddler, child or adult. A baby's emotions will swing around the balance point on the scale that has abject fear at one end and total unconditional love at the other.

How parents and other carers respond to the baby's emotional expression is crucial to its healthy development on all the levels of mind, body and spirit. Naturally, the mother has the most profound effect in the first few months, and how she reacts to the expression of love and fear in its varying degrees will set the scene for the way the child learns to handle its emotions in the years to come. Every adult response to the child's emotional expression contributes to that child's emotional education. Respond consistently with love and acceptance and you will help the child grow into an emotionally intelligent human being. Respond to their love with rejection, to their fear with disapproval, to their anger with fear, and you will have a profound effect on what the child takes in as being acceptable and unacceptable.

The effect of emotional mismanagement is not confined to the emotional sphere. Unaccepted emotions can be suppressed and kept inside, affecting all other aspects of growth and development. Emotions are flows of energy. If their expression is blocked, the energy has to find other ways to dissipate. It is likely to do this through physical, spiritual and mental paths, which adversely affects the growth of the body, the development of attitudes and beliefs, and the connection to the spiritual realms that is so important for the wholeness of the human self.

Can You offer some specific guidance as to how we can encourage emotional health and understanding, given that most of us are not fully emotionally intelligent ourselves?

The process of aiding the healthy emotional development of babies and children is very simple, even if not so easy to put into practice. Respond to every aspect of a child's emotional expression with love and acceptance. At the level of **emotions**, be ready to agree that anything goes. And be very clear that this does not mean that anything goes at the level of **behaviour** in acting out the emotions.

When children are bubbling over with love, accept and acknowledge that love, help them to savour it and to express it in ways that enhance the experience. Help them to relish the experience, to come to understand what triggers it, where they feel it inside them, what words they can learn to express it, how they can show it through their play, their creativity, their behaviour to others. Help them to experience the source of that love as both inside themselves and coming from Me. Help them to understand the positive effect that their loving feelings can have on themselves, on others and on the energy around them. The effect can be far greater than most of you can imagine. Use the process of helping your young to come to an understanding of love to gain what you may not have received when you were a young child. See the effect of their powerful and unconditional love on all life around them, and enjoy for yourself the experience of being so totally loved.

When your children feel fear, accept and acknowledge that this is what they are feeling. Help them to understand the source of it, to find the words and acceptable actions to express it. Help them to know that they can be safe even as they experience the fear, so that the experiencing of it is not debilitating. Avoid leaving them alone in it. Ignore everything you have ever read or been told about leaving your children to cry. Crying is very good for them, it is an immensely releasing process that you could all be more free with. And the most useful way to cry and let out the fear, pain or hurt is to do it cradled in the arms of someone who really loves you, not all alone shut away in a room, excluded from the love of family members.

Give them the total unconditional love that will allow them to reach the point of choosing between fear or love. They can usefully learn that they have the choice, and how to make that choice. They can only do this if they are free to experience both emotions, and helped to feel safe enough to make the choice for themselves. The intense love and acceptance of someone they love completely is the best way of easing the process.

I trust you are getting the gist of what I am offering you here. It goes for all the range of emotions, both primary and secondary, that a child will experience and experiment with. Banning emotions, denying their existence, encouraging the child to act them out incongruently – all these things do considerable damage to their hearts, souls, bodies and minds.

It is hard to make the shift as parents. It can take a lifetime to come to a full understanding of the emotional elements of life, even if you have had an emotionally healthy upbringing. This is another reason why in highly evolved societies the young are guided through their early lives by the elders of the community, rather than just their parents.

As a society, you could put much more effort into correcting the ineffectiveness of previous generations of parenting by helping those about to become parents to heal their own emotional wounds. Provide young adults with the help and support necessary to develop their emotional intelligence to the point when they are ready to bear children of their own. Whilst you operate a compulsory education system that holds young adults in schools, you have the opportunity to educate them in such matters at an early age. Such a practical emotional education would stand them in much better stead than many of the academic subjects you currently expose them to.

For those who are already parents and are struggling with the whirlwind of emotions that your children experience and which are triggered in you as a result, you can seek help from those more in touch with, and understanding of, the full range of human emotions.

Recognising that you have much to learn about emotions, and many unuseful old patterns to undo, is one of the signs of greatest strength in a human being. It is possible to rate the overall intelligence of your national cultures by the degree to which they a) experience and accept the full range of human emotions and b) accept that it is appropriate to ask for help in learning about such things.

Above all remember that your children can be your teachers in this area as in so many others. Develop your ability and willingness to empathise with your children's emotional states and you will have plenty of opportunity to heal your own emotional upbringing.

To empathise with your children means to combine a detachment from them with sharing some level of the emotional experience they are going through. It is almost like trying to place a small element of yourself in their shoes, to experience what they are experiencing, without getting so sucked into your own feelings that you cannot remain objective. I emphasise this notion of detachment, for it is truly unuseful for a parent to become so associated with their child's feelings that they take them on as their own. More appropriate is to aim for personal involvement without emotional involvement. Then you can be fully present for the child with some sense of what they may be feeling, yet detached enough to be effective in helping them through the experience.

The American family therapist Virginia Satir[8] once described empathy as "walking in another person's shoes with the laces undone".

There have been many wise people living on your planet in the recent past. Perhaps it is time for the lessons they have to teach to become more generally known.

13. Teenagers

The moment of transition from child to adult is quite clearly defined in biological terms, and involves the sexual maturation of the human body. For many this physical maturation happens before they enter the "teen" years. In traditional societies at this stage the child has now become an adult, preparation for adult life is complete and life alongside other adults now begins. This has changed in those human societies where the emphasis is placed on intellectual schooling rather than on learning through living fully in the world.

Herein lies the root of many of the problems you face with adults of this age group. Whilst you continue to deny these young adults the full range of opportunities they need for their social and emotional maturing, you will always have significant problems with disaffection.

The years that follow the sexual maturing of the human being are those in which he or she seeks to discover what it is like to live as an adult. This is the time of experimenting and exploring, testing and seeking. Give young adults a place in the world alongside other adults and they will be more than adequately exposed to the lessons of life and effective socialisation by their community. They can develop the attitudes, abilities and skills they need for themselves and which their communities also need.

Instead of which, what do you do?

You put these young adults together in institutions, keep them apart from the adult models they need, deny them full opportunities to explore and experiment, focus them on their minds to the detriment of their hearts, souls and bodies, and treat them as though they are still children.

The only extraordinary thing about this is that they do not all rebel a lot more than they do at present.

Your "teenagers" need to live and work alongside living and working models of how to **be** and what to **do** in the adult world. Instead you replace real models with the images and fantasies portrayed through film and television.

Young adults need to learn to care and love in an adult way, separating from their primary carers and experimenting with their emotions and sexuality with the support of emotionally and sexually mature adults. Instead you throw them together to share all the confusion of physical, emotional and sexual feelings and what is deemed "right" and "proper" by the world they are as yet denied access to.

On the one hand you give them unclear guidance about what is acceptable social and sexual behaviour. On the other you expose them to erotic and violent fantasies that contravene much of what they have been told. At the same time, you are less than open and honest with them about your own feelings, sexuality and morality. It is hard for them to develop self-responsibility in their personal lives with so little valuable guidance and consistency from older generations.

As a parent I am feeling somewhat criticised!

I appreciate that it can be hard to face up to the reality of what you are doing. Many times I have sent messengers and teachers among you to encourage you to open your eyes and look at the world you are creating. Many times I have been so gentle as to fail to get through to you. Please accept that the toughness of this message is a sign of My great love for humanity.

There are many examples of effective living and good works around you. There are any number of individuals and a few communities that have opted to pursue a spiritual path without being restricted by either religion or society. You can seek out such people and communities for the beneficial models they can provide.

I want to bring you a message of hope, to show you that there is another way to **be** in the world that will help you regain your spirits and start moving again towards the evolution of human consciousness. I cannot bring you such a message without sharing with you the many observations I have about what is not working now. I need to share with you the reality of the present as well as the possibilities for the future. You can choose love over fear, heart and spirit over technology, and save your world and yourselves today. It will be hard to do if you continue with the patterns of the past that serve you so poorly.

Stay hopeful. Many people are beginning to turn their faces away from the golden idols of technology and consumerism and are seeking the truth in their hearts and souls and the land around them.

If your societies are not yet ready to abandon the belief in schooling for teenagers, you could shift the emphasis away from full-time schooling and academic instruction towards a part-time education relevant to life. You could combine this with working alongside fully-grown adults in the many areas of life in which teenagers could both add value and increase their learning.

Bear in mind that the most crucial lessons to reinforce, prior to young people reaching positions of responsibility in society, are those of love, care and compassion, a sense of oneness with all life, human and otherwise, and a sense of reverence for the wisdom of the land, of nature and of the elders.

It would not be wise to take hordes of young people out of schools and stick them in lifeless factories where none of these lessons could be learnt. It would make great sense to involve them in working on the land, in providing service to the aged, infirm and needy, and in serving their local communities through tending communal spaces and enhancing the aesthetic and spiritual qualities of their environment.

Such activities would most suitably make a genuine contribution to the community, rather than be created as some form of "job creation programme" to keep young people off the streets. They would bring a realistic financial return to all those involved, and engage young people in working alongside committed and enthusiastic adults lovingly engaged both in service to their communities and the guiding of their younger colleagues.

It would not be beyond the bounds of your collective creativity to develop "life-schools" with a curriculum of love and care, participation and exploration, where the classroom is the community, and where those people living and working in that community have some degree of involvement in guiding and nurturing the young.

In **On Life** we talked a little about ideas such as local monetary systems and other ways of breaking out of the domination of global business and currencies. A system of local life education could be partly funded through local exchange trading systems[9], keeping the energy generated through living, growing and education as much as possible within the communities where these take place.

What about the cry for academic achievement, educational success, preparing for higher-level education?

You have examples in your world of people who manage to combine real-life education with academic achievement for those who want it. Explore some of the more radical attempts at secondary education in countries like Denmark, where a few schools have been built around practical activities and education for all, with those few who want to go to university achieving the required academic qualifications in months rather than years.

In chasing academic qualifications you are not serving yourselves or society. All you have done is to increase the competition and shift the goalposts. Soon not even one doctorate will be enough to secure employment, let alone an undergraduate degree. At one end of the scale the academic route isn't working, whilst at the other you have all but lost the vocational development for those who genuinely want to work with their hearts, souls and bodies more than their minds.

You can do something practical for and with the large group of disaffected young people currently lost in the teen years. You can help them go through the initiation into adult life by providing them with meaningful work, relevant training, emotional and spiritual guidance and the love and companionship of other adults including the elders of your communities.

In practice, how can we afford to do such things?

You currently spend thousands of millions of pounds in keeping young people in institutions that meet neither their own nor society's needs. The activities of all these potentially productive people can generate huge flows of energy and value in and around their local communities. Why should it be only the banks, supermarket chains and airlines that create their own money? Why could not local communities take on the role of creating currencies and wealth to benefit themselves and their future generations? It is all achievable if approached with love rather than with fear.

The "problem" of the teenage generation is one of your own making. And it is relatively easy to solve. Take a holistic approach to the concept of initiation into adult life, and you will find synergistic ways to better provide opportunities for teenagers and for the rest of the population as well.

To be able to make a start, as a society you need to be willing to abandon the fear that currently drives you to keep young people in schools rather than in the community where they belong. Replace the fear with the love of life, nature, yourselves and each other.

14. Rules and Controls

Living the lives that you do in your modern industrialised societies, rules and controls are necessary in the family, just as they are in the community at large. And, just as too many rules in the community deplete individuals' abilities to take responsibility for themselves and others, so do too many rules within the family.

In an ideal environment rules would not be required at all: controls would exist within the individuals and so would not have to be imposed externally. If you had the level of emotional and spiritual awareness now to fully live a life of love rather than fear, then you could bring up children to be sufficiently tuned into their own needs and those of others that they could not act against the interests of all. Then, rules and controls would not have to be imposed.

Rules and controls are necessary because you have not learnt to operate with total unconditional love. Whilst fear continues to guide you through your human existence lacking in spiritual awareness and self-acceptance, rules and controls will continue to be important. To remove them in the hope that this would lead to a change in attitudes and ways of being would be foolish in the extreme. The attitudes and ways of being need to shift so that they are governed by love rather than fear, and then the rules and controls will quite naturally fall away as they have no further use.

Part of beginning to help the young human beings in your families to learn to live with love instead of fear would be to encourage them to become self-controlling, so needing fewer rules and controls imposed by you.

Where parents feel that they need a set of rules in order to protect their children and the quality of their family life, then by all means impose them. Before you do so, take a good deal of time to decide how far the rules you choose to impose stem from a loving or a fearful place. Then examine how you intend to impose them or have already done so, not to mention the way you will police them, and ask again how far they come from a loving rather than a fearful attitude to life. This might well affect the number and types of rules you come up with for your family, as well as how you establish and maintain them and deal with any transgressions.

Are the rules designed to encourage a loving atmosphere of self-responsibility wherein young people are likely to agree their own sets of controls? Or are they designed to break the will of the children in your care and socialise them into fearful humans with little or no spiritual awareness? Controls that stem from the heart and soul will always be infinitely more effective at maintaining social order than rules that stem from the mind alone.

I said in an earlier chapter that the word "no" is sufficiently important to be used only when absolutely necessary. The same can be said of rules. Choose to set the absolute minimum number of rules and make them sufficiently important to be easy to accept and follow.

To do this effectively, you will need to differentiate between human needs and human wants. To give you some examples of what this means consider the following:

A teenager may **want** to stay out late at a party rather

than come home at the appointed hour. What they **need** may be to feel they belong, at this point in their peer group rather than their family. The parents may **want** them to be home at 10pm; what they **need** may be to know that their child will be safe.

Parents may **want** their children to watch less television. What they **need** is perhaps to feel that they are protecting them from violent and fearful influences. The children in question may **want** to watch all the programmes that their friends watch. What they **need** perhaps is to be credible in the eyes of their mates.

By looking beneath the presenting want and working with the underlying need, it is possible for parents and children of all ages to start to develop solutions for living together that meet all the needs in the family without necessarily satisfying all the wants. There are ways for children to remain safe and stay out late. There are ways for children to be credible in the eyes of their peers and not expose themselves to violent and fearful influences. There are ways for parents and children to all get their needs met and care for each other, if they do so from a position of love rather than fear.

What You are talking about is self-regulation through mutual caring rather than autocratic imposition. Yet isn't there a place for the firm imposition of non-negotiable rules? What about "tough love"?

Until such time as love becomes the norm rather than fear, and so brings about the transformation of the societies in which you live, there will be a legitimate place for the imposition of some rules and controls for the protection of life and limb. If you can choose and implement these rules with as much love and awareness as possible, you will minimise the negative effects of their imposition.

As to "tough love" – beware the risk of acting with great power from a fear base and convincing yourselves that you are doing it only out of love for your children. You may be. Yet if the core behind your use of power is fear, the chances are that your way of doing it will be fearful, not loving, and its effect on the recipients will also be fearful, not loving.

There is an important place for firmness in the loving relationship. You yourself have questioned some of what I have said in our writing so far as verging somewhat on the brutal. My response has been that sometimes to be loving you have to act with the compassion of the owl that strikes cleanly and silently in the darkness, shocking the "victim" into an altered state of being. If your motivation is truly loving and you act in a loving way, resisting the temptation to abuse your power over others, then firm, clean cuts can be infinitely loving.

Ultimately a significant question will be: do you love your children and teenagers enough to help them develop the self-responsibility rooted in self-love and compassion for all life that will lead them to a place where your rules become unnecessary? If you can truly answer yes to this question at the levels of heart, soul, mind and body, then you will be able to work with them to find the most effective ways to help them grow.

If the answer is no, if you are too fearful as yet to let them go and accept that they have their own lives to lead and are their own spiritual as well as human beings, then you have more work to do on your ability to love yourself and heal your separation from the spiritual and from Me.

15. Spiritual Education

Education is most useful if it is a holistic process. And of course it is whether you want it to be or not. Whatever you do, a child learns at all levels as he or she grows, even from before birth – learning about how to be in the world and about what is considered right and wrong. This learning takes place in the mind, in the heart, in the body and in the soul. Patterns of thinking, believing and feeling and of physical shape, form and doing are set up as a direct result of the unconscious education of the child by those caring for him or her.

This process would be very much more effective if it were not so strongly affected by the fear-thoughts and fearful culture that exist around the majority of children. To counteract this influence, it is increasingly important that the holistic education of children and young people is approached with much greater conscious awareness.

We have talked in earlier chapters about some elements of this; let us now talk about the specific element of spiritual education.

As a starting place, remember that you are all spiritual beings having a human existence, rather than not human beings some of whom may at some point have a spiritual experience. Long before the body was conceived and long after it has returned to the ground, your spiritual lives have existed and will continue to exist. You exist in this life right now as the aspect of your soul that chose to be incarnated in this body. As stated in our first book, the soul is in actuality far greater than that aspect of it that is incarnated in this body in this space/time. You may be incarnated in a variety of life forms at the same time, as well as living aspects of life at other places and times in the spiritual realms.

Right now, we are concerned with the education of the human in all things spiritual so that the soul is as involved as possible in the physical existence you are leading now. For too many of you, the soul features little, if at all, in your human lives. As a result, you miss out and your soul misses out. You are unable in this particular life to pursue the soul purpose that brought you here in the first place, so risking a degree of stagnation in the evolution of your overall spiritual consciousness.

The connection to soul is still strong during the early years of a child's life, strongest at the start and, unless encouraged, slowly weakening with time. Any open-hearted and open-spirited parent is likely to be aware of the spiritual nature of their child in the first few months after birth. As children grow and become more communicative, many of them will give signs of having some degree of spiritual experience and awareness.

I remember my second son as a small child talking about seeing people and things that weren't there as far as we were concerned. He could tell how someone was feeling by their colour, and picked up immediately on positive and negative energy in places. No doubt when he first went to school he was told not to imagine things, as he stopped talking about them from about that time on.

This is a common experience of many children whose connection to the worlds of spirit is denied by the adults who care for them.

If you are to encourage such connections, and help the child develop on the soul level, you would best be both positive about such experiences and proactive in the child's spiritual education. Even if you as parents have currently lost your ability to commune with the spiritual elements of life, you can help your children retain theirs. Even if you have lost your connection to Me through your own lack of spiritual education, you can help your children enhance the natural connection they bring with them. You can do this in a variety of ways.

Crucial in the process is helping your children grow up with a connection to, and understanding of, the natural world. I exist in nature all around you. The glory of the seasons, the birth of new life on the planet every spring, the beauty of the sounds, sights, smell and textures of the living world are all aspects of My presence in your lives. Helping your children to develop a reverence and love for all that grows on your planet, all the birds and insects and animals, will help keep open not just their souls but also their hearts.

Remember that a large part of the holistic education process is about building an understanding that **love is all there is**. The love that children naturally feel for small furry animals, and for the beauty of the natural cycle of life, helps to keep their hearts open so that they experience love flowing through them from Me as well as from you.

A conscious process on your part of helping them develop an awareness of the spirit realms is another important element of spiritual education. Help them to be open to the beings that choose to be their spiritual helpers. Help them to build connections to the angels that come amongst you and the "little people", as you often refer to the elemental spiritual beings who exist so widely on planet

Earth yet are denied by all "sound, rational people". You can introduce your children to the world of spirit through the use of ritual, which I will return to later in this chapter. You can also reinforce rather than deny their experience in this area of life. When they talk to you about what most adults would consider imaginary experiences, engage with them fully. Avoid rationalising what they are experiencing, leave their young minds to play with making what sense of it they need to – which is usually very little – and watch as they draw spiritual and emotional sustenance from realms you may not remember experiencing when you were a child.

Above all, help them to understand that you are all one with each other and with all life on the planet. This is best done not at the level of mind, but at the level of heart and soul. Take a lead from some of the "native" cultures of your planet such as the North American peoples who traditionally educated their children to understand that the animals and birds, trees and plants were all their brothers and sisters. Help them to be open to communication with these siblings of the natural world so that they develop the understanding that all life is connected.

In this whole process, encourage them to feel safe in My presence in all things. These wondrous little beings are still more closely connected to Me at birth than most adults will ever experience. Encourage them to be aware that the love they feel in their hearts for all that touches them is part of the Love of God that is the life-spring of the universe. Help them to understand and appreciate that I am always beside them and that they can draw on Me for help and sustenance whenever they feel fearful or concerned.

Avoid the mistakes that your religions make in portraying Me as a judgmental God, so that they can determine for themselves what they think is right and wrong. For I love all living beings regardless of who they are, what they do, what they think or believe. The only "Day of Judgment" is in the minds of humanity, not in the reality of God. Too many of you judge and condemn yourselves and each other all the time, and so create hell on earth even though it does not exist as such in the spiritual realms.

Remember that in My eyes there is no right or wrong. In your worldly existence there are actions that work and ones that don't in your individual and collective journeying towards fulfilling the purpose of Life in the universe. The actions that work are not "right" any more than those that don't work are "wrong"; they just are. Teach your children to discriminate between effective and ineffective actions. They can do this simply by coming to an understanding of the full difference between love and fear. Truly loving behaviour works in the world, fearful behaviour does not.

Treat your children with love at all times. Resist the temptation to control them with fear. As we said in the chapter on Rules and Controls, this does not mean allowing them to get away with all kinds of behaviour that are not useful in the loving order of life. It means providing them with a model of how you believe they could most usefully behave, and accepting them unconditionally as they are, even as you work with them to develop ways of thinking, feeling and doing that are loving rather than fearful.

For those of you who have had no spiritual basis to your lives to date, having children and helping them to develop their own spiritual understanding is a wonderful opportunity to re-educate yourselves. Allow them to be your teachers as well as taking the teaching role when appropriate. They can help you open your hearts and souls to the spiritual reality of life on earth. They can introduce you to a felt experience of other spiritual life forms that do not incarnate on your planet but are nevertheless here with you.

What role does religion play in all of this?

As I have said before, particularly in **On Life**, the majority of the institutional religions of your current world are not serving the spiritual evolution of humanity. They have been effective instruments of social control through the ages, yet in so being they have largely lost their spiritual connections. There are many deeply spiritual people who are members of the various churches around the globe. And there are many people who have lost altogether their personal awareness of what it means to be deeply spiritual, substituting for this a belief in the rightness of their particular churches and their doctrines.

At this stage in the evolution of your planet and its life forms, it will be of far greater practical value for people to develop their own sense of the spiritual in all life and directly heal their sense of separation from Me. Most, though not all, of your religions are too enslaved by fear, too unloving, to be of great value in the urgent task of reawakening the spirit in humanity. Right now you need the message, not the institutionalised messenger; you need the teaching, not the school with its hierarchies and power games. You can get all this without the help of organised religion by opening your hearts and souls to Me and to the many spiritual helpers crowding around the planet at this critical time.

What can we do with our children to help them grow spiritually?

Spiritual education is fundamentally more about **being**

than **doing**, and you can usefully educate the being side through effective doing. One of the most effective tools you can use is the practice of reverence. Whatever you are doing, whether it is preparing a meal, walking in the park, playing or digging in the garden if you are fortunate enough to have one, invent and make use of ritual to cultivate a sense of reverence for the natural world, for the people you meet, for the essence of life in all things and for My love which connects you all together. Regularly give thanks in a ceremonial way for Life and all its bounty, for the connections you have to other people and other life forms, for the elements that make life possible, the sun and the wind and the rain, for the living planet on which you walk every day, and the joy in your hearts and the beauty than surrounds you.

You can use storytelling to introduce the spiritual dimensions of life through the power of myth and the imagination. Remember to focus on unconditional love and to avoid the many myths that exist in your various cultures, which have evolved through the use of fear to control and dominate the spirit.

Almost all your religious festivals have their roots in ancient wisdom. They developed at points in your calendar to fit in with the far older celebrations and rituals of the land, the harvest, the movements of the sun and the moon. Revive the reverence for life on planet Earth through rediscovering these older, wiser, appreciations of the planetary cycle of love and life. There is much spiritual wisdom around you: open your hearts and your minds and you will find people and books that you have either never noticed before or have dismissed as wacky or irreligious.

And finally, remember that education is a holistic process that you all go through all the time. Combine the spiritual with the emotional, the physical and the intellectual.

As we have said elsewhere, avoid over-stimulating the intellect in the first seven years or so of a child's life. Find ways to introduce the spiritual without turning it into a mental activity. Follow the natural lead of the child, who is after all closer to spirit that you are. Open yourselves to Me and trust the greater process of the Universe that is unfolding in your lives right now.

16. Sex and Sex Education

Let us open this chapter with a reminder about the chapter on Sex in **On Life**. People cannot be reminded too often about the power of spiritual love coursing between two human bodies in the act of sexual intercourse. When a man and a woman freely and lovingly engage in the energetic process of sexual excitement and its culmination in the union of heart, soul and body at the moment of orgasm, the total amount of love in their relationship and so in the world is increased.

Unfortunately the process of learning about sex is pretty much left to chance. Too many young people have to fumble around to find loving ways to pleasure each other. Learning the finer points of the erotic, emotional and spiritual aspects of lovemaking sometimes evades human beings for their whole lives.

So, I would very much advocate effective education about sex in its full beauty.

Rather than avoiding the issue of sex education, or restricting it to attempts to train young people in birth control, parents could valuably find it in themselves to overcome their inhibitions and engage their offspring in dialogue about sex. Tell young people about the potential joy and wonder of real lovemaking. Make them aware that it can be a deeply emotional and spiritual experience. Help them to fully grasp the concept of physical pleasure and how to make it as intense and enjoyable as possible.

This will be a problem for some people in some parts of the world, largely because of past sexual repression. However, if young people are to learn from the experience of their elders, sexual inhibitions need to be undone. It may be that if you cannot talk to your children about sex you can at least discuss it with some of your close friends, and find out who is able and willing to tell of their joyful and loving experiences. After all, sex education need not be carried out only by the parents.

It does seem incredible to Me that such a powerful and joyful act, so commonly practised in your world, is subject to so many taboos. I know that in some countries teachers have been heavily criticised for being "too open" with young people in their sex education; this alone might make people other than parents reluctant to involve themselves in the educational process lest they be condemned by those who cannot appreciate either the beauty or the importance of sex.

My observations are that you are dangerously free with models of sexual acts that stem from fear and violence. The negative images of current human sexual practice far outweigh the positive and loving images and insights that you could be portraying. You could redress the balance through open discussion, evocative literature and the use of film and video to help open up young people's understanding of what sex is all about and how much more it can be than just copulating.

What about the issue of sexual practice amongst young people? There are still many groups who advocate no sex outside marriage, even though in most parts of the world it is hard to hold on to your virginity long enough to get married! And this all raises again the issue of birth control and abortion.

As I said in **On Life**, if sex in the human was just about making babies I would not have given woman the ability to refocus her sexual energy once a month through the menstrual cycle. Once, twice or three times a year would have been more appropriate. For thousands of years women knew the secrets of becoming pregnant and avoiding pregnancy, and so were free to use their sexuality to tap into the Goddess, to connect directly with Me. This started to decline with the switch from a matriarchal, love-based society to a patriarchal fear-based one in which men sought to take over the connection with the Divine by inventing a vengeful, omnipotent God.

You have made it again to the stage in evolution that you so enjoyed as a species in older, wiser times, that allows for lovemaking without the burden of too many babies. It is unfortunate that some of the more technological methods of birth control have much worse physical side effects than the older natural – and just as effective – ways now lost to the majority. The freedom to use the sexual act as an act of loving and spiritual connection between two people, and to generate more love in the world, can be a valuable tool in the spiritual transformation of the planet. Use it wisely, and above all with great love.

Encourage its wise and loving use by young people as well as adults of all ages. Do not be held back by the social mores that arose in the so-called Dark Ages of western human history. Help the young to celebrate their humanness as much through their sexuality as through other activities. Teaching them about sex as a spiritual act can help them to develop great reverence and respect for themselves, each other and Me. It can open them up to a deeper understanding of care and compassion. It is through the act of spiritual, emotional and physical union with another in lovemaking that they will come to understand what it means to be one with others and with Me. Through the conscious act of making sexual love they will come most easily to appreciate the difference between being a spiritual being having a human existence, and being only a human being occasionally having a spiritual experience.

The process of implementing such radical changes in your attitudes to and practice of sex will require great wisdom and maturity. I am not advocating a sudden switch to the kind of free love scenario that results in physical promiscuity. Parents would not be wise to encourage their children to "sleep around" as some people put it. The art of lovemaking is a disciplined and mature activity that needs to be taken seriously, not just played with. So much so that, were it possible, I would advocate the subject as one of the most important for your educational curriculum in schools, as well as in the home.

You are telling us to encourage the young to learn about the spiritual, emotional and physical aspects of lovemaking when they are ready. You are not advocating uncontrolled free love of the promiscuous kind, but are You advocating young people to form sexual bonds at an early age which would take them on into marriage?

I am certainly not suggesting that sex should only be practised in long-term relationships. Quite the contrary. Provided you take a spiritual approach, spreading the lovemaking around will create deeper bonds between people in wider groups than nuclear families and can only help to increase the cohesion in your communities.

It is not particularly useful in community building for macho young men to be able to boast about the young women they have bedded, any more than it is for young women to boast about how many men they have successfully seduced. These are aspects of sex as a purely physical act that do little for the parties concerned or the community in which they live.

How different it would be if people could remember and maybe even at times talk about the great bonds they have built with other people in their communities through the deep care and shared passion, and the joy of spiritual intimacy experienced with others whom they can now count as their friends and loved ones, even if not in life partnership with them.

What about the possible negative physical consequences of all this loving sleeping around, in the form of Aids and other sexually transmitted diseases?

In the short term these present you all with continued risks. Aids is a classic fear disease. It can only ultimately be conquered by the application of love to individual relationships, to communities and society as a whole. As a disease it feeds on the fear that is prevalent in human society at this time. The more fearful you become and the more you act, organise, legislate and create out of fear, the more you open yourselves as a species to diseases of this kind. Above all, do not let such diseases stand in the way of acting with love. You can find ways around the short-term risks to the individual in order to generate the social love energy that is required to counteract and eventually eradicate such ailments of the collective human spirit.

And abortion?

Re-read Chapter Four! Abortion should seldom be necessary if sex education is effective and you rediscover some of the older wisdom about birth control. And it is never appropriate to rule out any path. You cannot end a human life without that person's soul agreement. Every death is chosen. Some souls choose to incarnate knowing that their purpose in this life is to heal the emotional state of the mother and/or father through giving their human life to right a mistake or provide a lesson. If abortion is necessary, focus on what the individuals involved need to learn from such a choice, rather than condemning them for the way they have unconsciously chosen to experience the lesson.

17. Separation and Divorce

I do recognise that much emotional pain and suffering accompanies the break-up of your nuclear families in those societies where a strong emphasis is placed on this form of unit. It is a real problem right now in most western industrialised countries, where you have long since lost the family and community support systems that might otherwise pick up the emotional and financial load.

As I said in the chapter on Marriage, it is not useful for you to assume that marriage is a state blessed by Me and meant automatically to be life-long. Really strong, long-term, intimate relationships take a considerable amount of regular effort to nurture as the partners in them grow. Without that, they will inevitably cease to serve either partner and will ultimately come to an end. There is nothing "wrong" in this. It is inappropriate to see separation and divorce as intrinsically bad. They are products of an unuseful way to look at life partnerships in the first place and the impractical way of caring for children that has developed in cultures based on the nuclear family.

To really change the negative effects of separation and divorce you will need to work towards changing the basis of marriage, family life and the nurturing of children. In highly evolved societies, the role of growing, nurturing and educating future generations is taken on by the community as a whole, with the special involvement of the elders. Living in spiritually-based tribes or community groupings would free you from the intense, hothouse effect of marriage as you now know it. It would both reduce the likelihood of painful separation and make staying together for the sake of the children somewhat irrelevant.

This is an ideal that you can work towards over many generations. In the meantime, there is much that you can do individually and communally to ease the burden of so many people right now.

The strain generated by separation and divorce owes most of its causes to fear – fear of financial hardship, fear of being blamed, fear of failure, fear of other people's opinions and judgments, fear of being alone and not being able to cope. The whole thing is seen as such a process of failure that there is little opportunity for love to shine through even when it perhaps still exists in the marriage.

The problem often lies in the fact that the love that binds two married or cohabiting people is not truly unconditional, and can easily turn to fear. As one starts to grow faster than the other, or in a different direction, instead of celebrating the signs of growth, the other starts to feel threatened and fearful. This leads to holding on more tightly and trying to restrict the growth that appears to be causing the problem. How much better it would be if the two people could celebrate each other's growth and help each other to move forward, even if in different directions. The paradoxical reality is that two people who both desire to grow and evolve emotionally and spiritually are far more likely to find ways to constantly rebuild and renew their relationship than to lose each other.

Change is the only thing of which you can be one hundred percent certain. You will be different tomorrow from what you are today or were yesterday. Human beings deny this too much of the time, constantly fighting to remain the same against all the forces of nature, let alone those of spirit. Enjoy the change that slowly but surely happens to each and every one of you as you grow. Celebrate it together, nurture it in each other, help and guide where you can, learn and support where you can't immediately help.

One of the most useful things you can do is to help to bring out the underlying love that brought you together in the first place. This is hard to achieve in the heat of a flaming row that comes months, if not years, after things first started to cease working between the two of you. If you have been unlucky enough to have been in a marriage where open and honest communication has been lacking for some time, you could undoubtedly do with some external help and support.

It strikes Me as strange that your societies claim to be so concerned about this issue and yet marriage guidance counselling services, where they exist, are strapped for cash and incapable of meeting the demand placed upon them.

If you can find a loving way to work through the differences between you, you have a far better chance of coming to an amicable ending of your relationship than if fear is the driver. This will then have a significant effect on the emotional aspects of the divorce or separation process.

The research into the break-up of marriages highlights the relative poverty experienced by the person left caring for the children. Is this alone not a reason for people to force themselves to stay together?

Staying together for the sake of the children almost

always means staying together for the sake of one or other spouse who is too terrified to deal with the consequences of being alone. Children can provide a perfect excuse for refusing to see the truth and acting lovingly and responsibly in its light.

The great poverty that many single parents experience in many western industrial countries today exists because society does not value the role of parenting enough, even though to do so would make sound economic sense. It exists because you do not invest enough in the development of effective parenting and the provision of adequate social and financial structures to support carers in your society. It is not caused by divorce.

And yet the cost of not doing anything positive for families in your communities is far greater than would be the cost of providing an adequate income and adequate social structures for families with children in the first place. It is always hugely more expensive to clear up a mess than to prevent one.

In many "rich" nations you have successfully built a culture in which it is almost impossible to maintain the "acceptable" standard of living without two parents going out to work. That means that the children in such families suffer the lack of a parent around to help them grow naturally in the world. At the same time, children in families where no-one works suffer because their parents are unable to provide anything like the "acceptable" standard of living. The huge inequities in your society cost you all very, very dear.

In a more highly evolved society, you would recognise that the job of guiding children through their first seven to ten years is too important to be left to people who may not love them totally. You would ensure that young people and prospective or new parents had adequate help and training to prepare for the emotional and spiritual aspects of their role. You would ensure that at least one adult family member – preferably much of the time two – had adequate financial resources to devote to being with the children without having to go out to work. You would provide enormous resources to ensure that local communities were family-friendly places, and that parents could themselves continue to grow and evolve alongside their children.

I can hear you saying, ah, but this would all cost a fortune. The fortune that is being lost is the spirit of your children, the very future of your society. It is just because you have made the process of raising children so cheap that you are facing enormous problems in every other aspect of life.

Value parenting enough and it would be possible for the bulk of couples who decide to get together and have a family to stay together. The cost of divorce and separation would plummet and your communities would be far happier places.

I am immediately caught up in thinking about ideas for basic income or tax credit[10], that would be paid to families with children so that only one parent would have to work, if that. There is a convincing theory showing how much cheaper it would be if everyone were paid a basic living wage and those that chose to earn considerably in excess of that were then taxed. How come we can't see that such things might work?

The reason is that you are still all operating in an entirely fear-based culture and something like that would be an eminently loving thing to do. The fear is of people sponging off the state, becoming a burden, dragging the system down. In reality, of course, it is the huge consumer power of the middle classes in work that places the burden on society and the planet, devouring your natural resources and working people to sickness and death in a feverish rush for economic growth and the false sense of well-being that it sets up as its golden calf.

Remember that young people are the greatest asset of your society. If you were to stop reproducing tomorrow, it would take only a very few years for the entire global economy to collapse completely. It makes no sense to devote so little of the enormous resources of your world to giving the young a good start in life. A big part of the problem lies in the misconception about what a good start would mean. You seem to be busy defining it as an intellectual education built on a consumerist lifestyle. You would do better to define it as a solid sense of the young person's spiritual being and a love for all living things in the universe. From these would stem all that they need to flourish in life.

Many of you are too busy filling your world and your lives with things you really don't need, at the expense of each other, the environment and the other living creatures on the planet, filling the emptiness within in the hope that you will thereby find salvation. You will only come to salvation by recognising that going through the emptiness within you is the way to find Me and each other again.

The current struggle many of you experience around the issue of separation and divorce stems as much from the lack of spirit and love in your relationships and your communities as it does from any economic or social causes.

How you go about separation and divorce is perhaps more important than the events themselves. The more acceptance of each other and yourselves you can muster the better. The more love you bring into the proceedings, the less trauma will result. The more openness and compassion you manage, the less hurt you will cause. The more respect you show each other and all the children, parents-in-law, siblings and so on, the more you will be able to reduce the emotional damage that might otherwise be inflicted on all concerned.

Society's attempts to help the process of divorce would be most effectively focused on these "soft" areas rather than on rewriting legislation, providing funding for matrimonial legal services and chasing absent parents for maintenance payments.

19. Bereavement and Death

Attitudes to death are reflected in the ways families act in the face of death, and are reinforced and passed on to new generations most powerfully through the family.

There was a time in your own society's history when the family was where you learnt all about birth and death. That has changed enormously over the last fifty years. In many parts of the less technologically developed world it is still the case, and for the millions of people in those areas, attitudes to death are very different and not as fearful as in your western societies.

Let us be clear that the problems so many people have with loss and bereavement stem from your current fear of dying. If you accepted that a) every death is chosen and b) death is only the end of the human condition and a release back into the spiritual realms, then death would be an occasion to mark, but not to mourn. As such, bereavement would be a process of coming to terms with living without your departed friends and relations in the light of knowing that they are moving on in their spiritual evolution.

You would enrich the life experience of everyone if you made death more a part of your lives, just as if you made birth more a part. Helping children and young people to learn about the spiritual, emotional and physical elements of leaving the body in relation to grandparents,

parents or close friends provides you with a glorious opportunity to further their spiritual education; at the same time it can counteract the message of fear they may otherwise pick up about death. A child's acceptance of death is quite natural until he or she is taught to fear it. And departed people often live on as joyous memories far more for children than for adults, who fail to come to terms with the death of people they love. This is because most young children have not learnt to be emotionally dependent on others in quite the same way as many adults have.

In the meantime, it would be helpful to make bereavement more of a spiritual process in the family, by bringing in simple rituals and activities both to celebrate the life of those departed and to acknowledge the sense of loss. As much as death is a release for the dying, it leaves an emotional hole for those remaining alive. The loss felt for a departed love one is real and can usefully be fully acknowledged as such. Allow yourselves to experience the grief as part of the letting go process. The feelings will be strongest when someone has been emotionally dependent on the person who has died and weakest, not in those who feel less, but in those who are strong enough in themselves to easily let go of those departing.

Least useful in the process of bereavement is the tendency many of you have to ignore or deny your feelings and get on with life regardless of the inevitable emotional changes that death brings. Equally unuseful are blame and anger, either directed at the dead, the living held responsible for death or the self who takes personal blame. These reactions are most usually the result of denying the reality that death brings a positive experience for the souls of those who leave. Help in understanding the spiritual aspect of death will aid most people to focus on their grief rather than feeling guilty or angry.

Children and young people will often take less time to grieve than adults, provided they are permitted the free expression of their full range of emotional reactions. If they live in a family where the expression of sadness, anger or grief is not allowed, they are likely to bottle up their feelings and end up either becoming dis-eased or acting out their unresolved feelings in behaviour that is not useful and probably not acceptable.

Parents and children can share their grieving process, ritualising the memory of those departed through creating simple shrines, through recounting stories of the person who has died, and sharing memories, both pleasant – and if necessary – unpleasant. It is not useful to immortalise someone in death as other than they were in life, so all aspects of a life are worth remembering, not just the "good" bits.

You can help children make a simple shrine out of photographs, favourite artefacts belonging to the deceased, natural objects of beauty and spiritual symbols such as icons, crystals, rocks and candles. You can devise simple family rituals around such shrines during the months of the inevitable grieving process, decreasing their significance as the sense of loss diminishes. All concerned will know when the time has come for the departed one to be counted amongst the ancestors or spiritual friends rather than still to be grieved over.

You have done yourselves a disservice by placing birth and death in the hands of "professionals" and removing both from the family environment. The disservice is not only to those dying and being born but to all the family members who could be learning just how natural the processes of birth, death and life really are. And, the family presents an excellent medium for healing this whole situation.

Isn't part of the issue that we focus on trying to keep people alive as long as possible, and so take them out of their homes into medical institutions rather than providing them with a loving family environment in which to die?

This is how you have handed death over to the "professionals" as something to battle against right until the end. There is the beginning of a move away from this trend in those countries where it has become prevalent. Some medical doctors are now accepting that there is a point at which care should be aimed at making people comfortable in their dying process rather than treating them so as to avoid the end as long as possible. And you could move even further towards this more natural way of dying as you become better able to discern the spiritual readiness of the soul to leave the body. In the chapter on Death and Dying in our first book we talked about this in connection with the issue of euthanasia.

It is possible for you all to grow to the point where a soul-level decision to leave the physical body could be accompanied by a conscious decision to die in a way that would not require the physical fight that results in pain, trauma, incontinence, incapacity and the many other aspects of modern, diseased death. Then there would be no home in the world where death could not take place surrounded by love, compassion and the celebration of a life well lived.

All such simple emotional and physical activities can help the bereaved, which is the important aspect of the dying process. As we said in **On Life**, it is not dying that is a problem, but living. Shifting your attitude towards the spiritual will help you all to accept the natural and inevitable fact of death in your lives and allow you to rejoice when loved ones leave to continue their spiritual adventure in seeking eventual reunion with Me.

19. Old Age

There are many yardsticks by which you can assess the spiritual evolution of a society. One is how effective it is in ensuring that the fundamental needs of all its members are met. What you can see around you in your own country and many other "developed" ones is a decline in providing for the needs of the young and the old. We have talked quite a lot about the needs of the young, so in the twilight chapters of this book it is appropriate to talk about those of the old.

It used to be true that the greatest resource for the future of your societies was the young, whilst the greatest resource for the present was the old. So much wisdom, maturity, skill and common sense were contained in the heads and hearts of your older generation that elders were a great gift to their communities.

This has largely changed as a result of your love affair with technology. Technological change has happened so fast that older people are being left behind in their hundreds of thousands, and the knowledge, understanding and skills they have developed over a lifetime often seem irrelevant to the technophiles of the moment.

This current reality does not serve you well. You are losing the sense and sensibilities of the people who could best help keep you on course.

Many of the problems you face today stem from the fact that dynamic young entrepreneurial types, who do not have the wisdom and maturity of life behind them, are developing and implementing new technology without adequate consideration for its consequences. They are hooked on the technology bug and are in too much of a hurry to seek counsel from their elders, whom they dismiss as unlikely to understand. It is not technology that they need to seek counsel about from those with greater life experience and maturity: they need their help to anticipate and take seriously the effects of technological advances on all aspects of life.

A spiritually evolved society would treat its older people very differently from the way you now do in many parts of your world. Individuals would be valued for their contribution to the community, to productive work, to the role they have to play in the formal and informal education of the young and the not so young, as well as the many tasks that open-minded and open-hearted people who have lived a long time in a place are best equipped for.

We have already said that the grandparent generation is in many ways the one best suited to guide children and young people through their early years. In many truly civilised societies, the role of teacher is bestowed on those the community most respects for their life-long ability to grapple with the issues of life; it would never be offered to someone fresh out of teacher training college with no experience of life and work.

No spiritually evolved society would isolate its older generations from everyone else, any more than it would collect children up together in schools. Instead it would make sure that old and young, as well as all those in between, can live and work side by side within sustainable communities where personal and collective responsibility would be the order of the day.

To bring about change, a huge shift has to happen in personal and collective attitudes. Right now, fear of the "problem" of the increasing number of old people in many of your societies is keeping you from even thinking about how you could all start to address the issues. What is required is a shift from fear to love, a shift in ways of feeling and thinking, so that older people become valued for all they have to contribute rather than being seen as past it, or less than able to contribute in your rapidly changing world.

At a very personal level real change would involve a shift away from the gulf between the generations in families towards the potential for shared care and learning that could come from many generations of families living together in the same community, if not actually under one roof. This would no doubt require a shift in the attitudes of all generations.

Unconditional love as the norm would enable grandparents to be much more accepting of their children's lifestyles and to relate better to their offspring. Unconditional love on the part of the middle generations would allow them to heal the possible pain of their own childhood and to value the experience and maturity of their parents, uncles and aunts without holding on to their early hurts.

When you can be liberated from the fear and blame that gets in the way of so many adult parent and child relationships, you will come to realise that all the generations have much to contribute to each other all the way from birth to death.

At a broader social level, attitudes could similarly do with shifting in those societies where the elderly are no longer valued. There are models around the world for more effective ways to think about old people, even though so many urbanised societies are suffering the same problems of a growing proportion of non-productive members. The attitudes that you might sensibly seek to transform include attitudes to work and the western industrial model of production that sets an arbitrary age to retire. Such changes will require a shift in focus away from employment and monetary reward as the only measures of an individual's worth.

There is much that you need to do in your communities which you have convinced yourselves you cannot afford to do, and so many people available that you equally believe you can't employ. It would be possible with a little imagination to re-invent the way you live to find useful contributions for everyone willing and able to make them. It would take a radical rethinking of your dependence on economic theories devoid of heart and spirit.

You could make a huge difference to the quality of life of older people and their ability to take an active part in their communities if you relieved them of the anxiety of financial hardship. I question how it is possible for any society that considers itself civilised to treat old people as you do in many of your industrialised countries.

Not only do we treat old people in ways that devalue them and their contribution during their working lives, but we are ourselves so scared of old age that we are constantly looking for ways to avoid the inevitable.

This is another attitude that it would serve you well to let go of. The processes of ageing and dying could not be more natural. They do not have to be accompanied by pain, disability, loneliness and despair. These are elements of the process you have invented for yourselves. Becoming aware that you make your own choices about every aspect of your life, and that you can live in good health right up until the moment of choosing to die, could free you from the fear of ageing. Knowing that you do not have to buy into the prevailing attitudes that make people almost obsolete as they grow old will encourage people to retain their effectiveness and productivity even outside the economic spheres of life.

Current attempts to find technical fixes for the "problem" of growing old will never succeed. The fix is waiting for you in your hearts and souls. Shift your attitudes and beliefs, open your hearts, and old age can become a time of great joy and enlightenment rather than the dismal twilight of an earthly lifetime.

20. Ancestors and Tradition

As in many areas of life, this is a topic that requires a careful degree of balance. It is possible to be too hung up on traditions and past practices that prevent the steady evolution of ways of being and doing in the world. And it is possible to completely discount the wisdom of previous generations to the detriment of the present. In your rush for technological development these past fifty years or so, many of your societies around the planet have erred on the side of discounting the past to the point where you have lost much of the valid spiritual and environmental wisdom that your ancestors amassed. You have done so to the point where you are consequently at grave risk.

Increasing numbers of people are turning to new versions of the older ways of relating to spirit and the environment with which your ancestors were much more familiar than you. The re-emergence of interest in shamanism and ancient tribal wisdom is one good example. Another is the recognition that you have much to learn about how to care for planet Earth from traditional tribal peoples. There is much to be gained through such approaches, as well as others yet to be re-discovered.

Traditions are valid seeds for modern ideas. They do not of themselves always fit with the rapidly changing aspects of human life at the beginning of your twenty-first century, so they need adaptation. However, you will lose much if you disregard them completely.

An interesting point to consider is how to discern a valid tradition from an invalid or not useful one. After all, not all traditions are useful. There are some quite inappropriate customs still practised around the world that have grown up as traditions and held to steadfastly. You could do well to actively discard these and replace them with more humane and spiritual practices.

Now you have a very simple test to apply in such matters. Have the traditional practices you are considering developed out of love or out of fear? Those that cause individuals or sections of communities to suffer, that damage the environment, create competition and power games, and hold some people above others, will certainly have developed in the dim and distant past as a result of the fears of one element of society or another. These will not serve you well today as they have probably not done in the past.

Seek out the more spiritual traditions that have escaped being institutionalised or turned into rigid dogma, and see how they apply in modern circumstances. It is not surprising that many of the old spiritual teachings of the east have become popular in the north, south and west. The ancient traditions of the Orient, which grew up with little or no direct religious structures attached to them, have survived to be as relevant in the modern era as they were in years gone by.

What about family traditions?

Family traditions are perhaps a little less useful than more general cultural traditions. Traditions, and the traditional wisdom that has grown up over centuries, if not millennia, have already stood the test of time and weathered the criticism of philosophers and the general public. Family traditions that perhaps only date back a few generations may well have developed out of the power and dogmatism of a family patriarch or matriarch without being exposed to the critical testing of unrelated thinkers. As such they may be completely inappropriate now, even if they were appropriate in the past.

And you can apply the same test to them – love or fear? There are only ever two choices.

How does this whole consideration of ancestors relate to matters spiritual and the issues of timelessness that You have introduced us to? If time does not exist in a serial form and the physical human condition is only an aspect of the existence of the soul, are not our ancestors with us now, and can we not interact with them for guidance in this life?

In many traditional tribal societies this is precisely what happens. Reverence for the ancestors helps to keep a channel open between the spirits of the ancients and the hearts and souls of those alive in your world right now. There is much to be gained in maintaining strong connections with the wise who have lived before you – not to give up control or responsibility for your own lives, but so that you can seek their counsel in thinking through the most effective ways to live today.

There is much guidance available to you as to how to do this. The use of prayer and meditation in seeking counsel from the spirit realms is well understood and regularly written about. You can set aside some area of your family home in celebration of the ancestors in general, adorning it perhaps with symbols and representations of your personal ancestors and other spiritual artefacts. Providing a focus in this way for the spirits of the ancestors can help you and those who wish to be close to you to communicate effectively. Opening your hearts and souls through ritual and prayer to contact with those who have walked this planet before will also help you tap into the well of inner knowledge that every one of you brings into your earthly lives from your other existences.

There is no better way to introduce your children and young people to spiritual practice than to expose them to the celebration of the lives of their ancestors and the process of seeking wise counsel from the spiritual realms. Every child would benefit from an appreciation of the spiritual guides that are available to those who choose to make contact with them. You are all surrounded all the time by spiritual beings willing to help you in the struggles you have invented for the human condition. Make use of them yourselves, and help your children to come to love and appreciate the support that they can find from this direction.

Concern for your ancestors and for a sense of tradition can also show itself in an appreciation of human history. There is much to be learnt about how to live effectively in the present through studying aspects of the past. You can learn from past mistakes as well as how to adapt old traditional practices for current needs. On one level, education is only about remembering what you already know. The sum total of human understanding exists in the history of your planet. You have been through all of today's life-threatening situations before. If you could but tap into the great knowledge that is to be had on planet Earth you would be helped to find the answers to every issue facing you now.

Much has been lost. Yet more is available and kept obscure if not actively hidden. Ancient treasures of wisdom do exist in the world, many of which contravened the accepted social and religious order of the last many centuries. This wisdom has been secreted away and in some cases destroyed. As you move forward, there will be considerable pressure applied to bring such sources to light again. Humanity needs all the help it can get right now. As your churches and your governments come slowly to realise that the old order needs to change and that they don't have a monopoly on designing the future, they will be forced to make public the existence of great works of ancient wisdom that will stun historians and people the world over.

Tapping into ancient wisdom is not just an intellectual exercise. As I have said above, in seeking counsel from your ancestors you can also tap into the spiritual wisdom of the ages that belongs to you all. In finding your Oneness with Me and all life in the universe, you will be able to draw on the collective spiritual wisdom of Life itself. The channels for this lie in your heart and soul, not in your eyes and ears.

You also have access to the most established earthly ancestor of them all, and that is the planet itself. Great wisdom and counsel exist in the spirits of the natural world. The trees and rocks are your ancestors, not just the humans that have come before. Other life forms have much to teach those who will listen. The great mammals of the sea in particular have unbounded wisdom ready to share with those who can heal the rift your forbears created between you. Even for those of you not yet ready in evolutionary terms to communicate directly with the many life forms on your home planet, there is much simple and profound wisdom to be had from observation of the natural world.

Gaia and her creatures have talked to humans since

the beginnings of time. For tens of thousands of years you were adept at listening. This is a great art that you would do well to recover.

Know that it is time to remember your human and earthly ancestors. It is time to re-member yourselves, and become one again with the greater aspect of your past, your ancestors and the Oneness that is Me and Life in the universe.

Epilogue

Much of what We have talked about in this book is of vital importance for the future of humanity. By changing the way you guide your children through their growing up you will take a big step towards recovering from the path you have been following.

Treat children and young people at all times with love; bring them up in a world that is loving rather than fearful. Help them to develop their abilities to love and care for all life. Encourage them to develop compassion and respect for themselves and all living beings. Help them to fill their heads with loving thoughts, their bodies with nourishing food and their souls with the Love of God, and all will be well in the world to come.

Remember that quotation inspired by Me from *The Prophet* by Kahlil Gibran[11], that your children are not your children, they are the products of life's longing for itself. Treat them as spiritual beings having a human experience who start this particular life in your care and so require you to help them to the very best of your ability to be themselves, not an extension of your own longing for life.

Remember also that families are not all about children. Every parent is also a child. Every parent has a parent themselves to continue to be friends with, to love and be loved by. Your whole sense of family would shift in the West if you could find a new way to expand its boundaries beyond only two generations. You are at a point when people reaching maturity are no longer much valued in the industrialised workplace. You now have the opportunity to develop a renewed role for the elders of your families and communities so that they can involve themselves in guiding the next generation.

Involving the grandparents of your world in supporting the family process would do a lot to remove the stresses and strains now felt in many marriages and partnerships in which children are involved. Parents do not have to do it all alone. The effective nurturing and guiding of young people of all ages is too important to be left to one or two adults, themselves still learning and growing in life.

The last major social revolution in the industrialised world has contributed to the near destruction of the family as a viable place to bring up children. The next social revolution could start within the family and impact upon the whole world.

Anything is possible with love. And when the going gets tough, it would be valuable to remember that you are all one family anyway, and that I am both the Father and the Mother. Find a place for Me in your hearts and you will become open to each other on a scale you can only previously have dreamt of.

If you have reached the end of this book without having read **God Speaks On Life**, I urge you to read it before you move on to the subsequent books. This collection of books forms a holistic exploration of life in the round. You cannot afford to ignore any one aspect of it since it is all interconnected. The message will widen and deepen as you read On Life, On Work, On Community and On Society.

It is My intention to provide you with much food for thought, so that your appetite will be stimulated and you will expand and deepen your diet when you have eaten your fill of **God Speaks**. This wake-up call is designed to help you to realise that the direction you are taking needs to change and to know what you have to do to change it. Thereafter, you may or may not wish to go deeper into any one of the host of subjects we will touch upon by the end of our fifth book.

Come to Me now in the recognition that through the Love of God shared between all humanity you can find the way to live life to the full as a spiritual, not just a human experience. Through choosing a spiritual path you have the chance to avoid the ecological and social disasters that are gathering on the near horizon. It is My will that you make the necessary shift in consciousness: let it also be yours.

I love you so.

Notes

1   *A Course in Miracles*, Foundation for Inner Peace, USA, 1975
2   *Conversations with God*, Neale Donald Walsch, Hampton Roads Publishing, USA, 1995, Hodder and Stouton, UK, 1997
3   See *Co-Housing*, by C McCamant and C Durett, Ten Speed Press, USA, 1989 as well as contact The Cohousing Network, P. O. Box 2584, Berkeley, CA 94702, www.cohousing.org
4   Floris Books and Hawthorne Press, both UK based publishers specialise in books for parents and children that contain a spiritual element. They are readily obtainable around the world.
5   Steiner Schools fellowships exist in most countries. **In the UK** you can find information on local schools by writing to: Steiner Waldorf Schools, Kidbrooke Park, Forest Row, Sussex, RH18 5JA. **In the USA**, contact AWSNA Office, 3911 Bannister Road, Fair Oaks, CA 95628. **In NZ**, contact P. O. Box 888, Hastings, New Zealand.
6   There are many useful books. You might start with: *Getting to Yes*, Roger Fisher and William Ury, Hutchinson & Co, U.K., 1983. *P.E.T. Parent Effectiveness Training*, Thomas Gordon, New American Library, U.S.A., revised 1990
    Parenting Matters, Sheila Munro, Hawthorne Press, UK, 1998
    The Secret of Happy Children, Steven Biddulph, Bay Books, Australia, 1988
7   *Emotional Intelligence*, Daniel Goleman, Bloomsbury Publishing, UK, 1996; Bantam Books, USA, 1997
8   *The New People Making*, Virginia Satir, Science & Behavior Books, USA, 1988
9   One of the best books on LETS is *LETS Work – Rebuilding the Local Economy*, Peter Lang, Grover Books, UK, 1994
10 Information on such ideas can be had **in the UK** from Citizens Income Trust, St Philips Building, Sheffield Street, London, WC2A 2EX, www.citizens-income.org.uk; **in the USA** from Banneker Centre for Economic Justice, 5465 High Tide Court, Columbia, MD 21044, www.progress.org/banneker; **in NZ** UBINZ, c/o PSA, Private Bag 11-042, Palmerston North, www.geocities.com/ubinz.
11 *The Prophet*, Kahlil Gibran, Phone Media, USA, 1996; Pan, UK, 1991

About the author

Ivan Sokolov was born in 1953 of an English mother and White Russian father, and raised on a farm in England. He has had a varied career, including working as a fisherman, a community worker and local government officer, and running his own business before taking up training and facilitation in the early 1980s.

He pioneered parent education on a large scale in the United Kingdom, setting up a national charity with his second wife, Jacquie, to support parents with their family relationships.

Ivan was active in developing the Scott Peck approach to Community Building in Britain and it was this that, in the early 1990s, set him on the path of working at supporting business leaders to adopt humanistic and spiritual values within their companies. Since 1995 he has run his own consulting firm in this field, which has evolved into a successful partnership that dares to work openly from a spiritual perspective with client companies. Since his dialogue with God began, he has been following a path of service by bringing the message in **God Speaks** to as wide an audience as possible.

Ivan is married to Jacquie, who has also been his business partner since they met in 1984. They have shared their spiritual journey together over much rough as well as smooth terrain. They have a son born in 1994, while Ivan also has two grown-up sons by his first marriage. Ivan and family currently live in Bath, England, though they are soon to move to New Zealand, Jacquie's home country.

As well as doing executive coaching, team and organizational facilitation work, Ivan is a non-executive director of two commercial companies, and trustee of several small charitable foundations. When not working, his favourite pastime is spending time with his family out of doors and as close to nature as possible.

Other books in this collection

On Life   God Speaks on Life

The first book in the collection offers the fundamental message of **God Speaks** that is then expanded on in the rest of the books.

Chapter headings
On the Nature of God
The purpose of life
Soul
Emotions
Love and Fear
Relationships
Personal responsibility
Illness
Death and dying
Health, diet and exercise
Dreaming and sleep
Gender
Sex and erotic love
Religion
Prayer and meditation
Manifestation and creating
Money, wealth and abundance
Violence
Epilogue on suffering

Published in paperback at $12.95 US, £7.95 UK and $22.50 NZ. Available from bookstores, mail order on 1-800-431-1579 in the USA, 0117 942 0165 in the UK and 03 332 4089 in NZ. Direct from the publisher via the Internet or using the order form in the back of this book.

ISBN 1 903162 00 9

Book Three   God Speaks on Work
Available summer 2000

The dialogue continues, the style remains the same, while
the focus shifts to the workplace, with the emphasis on
corporations and profit making enterprises, though with
much relevance to non-profits, government departments
and any work context.

Chapter headings
Introduction
Work
Business
Motivation
Organization
Ownership and capital
Profit
Balance between work and home
Relationships at work
Emotions at work
Gender at work
Equal opportunities
Ethics at work
Spirituality at work
Management
Flexibility
Innovation and creativity
Leadership
Sustainability
The market place
Epilogue

Published in paperback at $12.95 US, £7.95 UK and $22.50
NZ. Available from bookstores, mail order on 1-800-431-1579
in the USA, 0117 942 0165 in the UK and 03 332 4089 in
NZ. Direct from the publisher via the Internet or using the order
form in the back of this book.

ISBN 1 903162 02 5

Book Four   God Speaks on Community
Available autumn 2000

The dialogue continues, the style remains the same, while the focus shifts away from the personal and the family to the local communities in which we live.

Chapter headings
Introduction
Inter-dependence
Neighbourliness
Caring
Equality
Racial tension
Personal responsibility
Competition
Housing
Money
Churches/religion
Local participation
Politics
Economics
Trade
Rules and control
Policing
Non-human life
Nature and the environment
Epilogue

Published in paperback at $12.95 US, £7.95 UK and $22.50 NZ. Available from bookstores, mail order on 1-800-431-1579 in the USA, 0117 942 0165 in the UK and 03 332 4089 in NZ. Direct from the publisher via the Internet or using the order form in the back of this book.

ISBN 1 903162 03 3

Book Five   God Speaks on Society
Available winter 2000

The dialogue continues, the style remains the same, while the focus shifts away from the local communities in which we live to the national and global level.

Chapter headings
Introduction
Leadership
Politics
Business
International relations
Globalisation
Disaffection
Violence
Policing
Armaments
Agriculture
Ecology
Sustainability
Health and dying
Education
Money
Pollution
Environmental responsibility
Science and research
Insurance and pensions
Conclusion

Published in paperback at $12.95 US, £7.95 UK and $22.50 NZ. Available from bookstores, mail order on 1-800-431-1579 in the USA, 0117 942 0165 in the UK and 03 332 4089 in NZ. Direct from the publisher via the Internet or using the order form in the back of this book.

ISBN 1 903162 04 1

Help spread the message

If you believe the message in this book is important, help spread it by telling your friends, giving them books, or ordering in bulk to sell in your local community. On the following pages you will find order forms that copy or remove and use. Substantial discounts are offered for purchases of 20 books or more.

Ordering books over the Internet

Books can be ordered from anywhere in the world and posted anywhere in the world from the publisher via the Internet. Orders are processed through secure encryption to the highest standards to ensure security of credit card information.

http://www.soulfodder.com

Ordering books by post or telephone

North America
Book Clearing House, 46 Purdy Street, Harrison, NY 10528
Telephone 1-800-431-1579 Fax 914 835 0398

UK and Europe
éco-logic books, 10-12 Picton Street, Bristol, BS6 5QA, UK
Telephone 0117 942 0165 Fax 0117 942 0164

NZ and Australia
Felicia House, 94 Opawa Road, Christchurch 8002, NZ,
Telephone 03 332 4089 FAX 03 332 4020

Suppliers in other areas will be detailed on the Soulfodder website as they become available – www.soulfodder.com.

Compact Disk for study

To aid the process of personal study, all the *God Speaks* books will be available on one CD in a searchable text form. This will make it easy for you to find sections of the text from all five books when you wish to revisit the content. Publication date for the CD is expected to be April 2001, so contact us for further information.

Soulfodder Press   Email: info@soulfodder.com

Workshops

To help you make the *God Speaks* message part of your life, Ivan Sokolov and a team of high calibre facilitators, with channelled input from God, are designing a two-stage workshop process. If reading any of the books in this series spurs you on to want to change your attitude to life and your way of being and doing in the world, yet you find change hard, these events will provide just the practical help you need.

To find out about the availability of these workshops at a venue near you, contact Soulfodder, by mail or email:

Soulfodder in USA
c/o 234 North Road, Fremont, New Hampshire NH 03044
Email: eventsUSA@soulfodder.com

Soulfodder in Europe
c/o Speke House, Long Beach Road, Longwell Green, Bristol, BS15 6UA, U.K. Email: eventsUK@soulfodder.com

Soulfodder in Australasia
C/o Felicia House, 94 Opawa Road, Christchurch 8002, New Zealand, Email: eventsNZ@soulfodder.com

Contacts in other areas will be detailed on the Soulfodder website as they become available – www.soulfodder.com

God Speaks on Family

Please send me:-

_____ copies of God Speaks on Family
@ £7.95 / US$12.95 / NZ$22.50   _____

Post and packing per book
US $3.50
Canada $7.95   Add p & p   _____
UK   £1.50
Europe   £2.00
All other   £3.00
NZ   NZ$3   Total _____
Australia   NZ$10

I enclose a cheque/International money order   y / n

Please charge my card — please circle: Visa   MasterCard

				Expires		

Name and address & **telephone number** of cardholder

_____

_____

_____

_____

Name and address to send books to if different from above

_____

_____

_____

_____

Make cheques payable to and send orders to:
North America
Book Clearing House, 46 Purdy Street, Harrison, NY 10528
UK, Europe and rest of the world
éco-logic books, 10-12 Picton Street, Bristol, BS6 5QA, UK
NZ, Australia
Felicia House, 94 Opawa Road, Christchurch 8002, NZ

God Speaks on Life

Please send me:-

_____ copies of God Speaks on Life

@ £7.95 / US$12.95 / NZ$22.50 _____

Post and packing per book

US	$3.50		
Canada	$7.95	Add p & p	_____
UK	£1.50		
Europe	£2.00		
All other	£3.00		
NZ	NZ$3	Total _____	
Australia	NZ$10		

I enclose a cheque/International money order   y / n

Please charge my card — please circle: Visa   MasterCard

Expires

Name and address & **telephone number** of cardholder

_____

_____

_____

_____

Name and address to send books to if different from above

_____

_____

_____

_____

Make cheques payable to and send orders to:

North America

Book Clearing House, 46 Purdy Street, Harrison, NY 10528

UK, Europe and rest of the world

éco-logic books, 10-12 Picton Street, Bristol, BS6 5QA, UK

NZ, Australia

Felicia House, 94 Opawa Road, Christchurch 8002, NZ

God Speaks on Work

Please send me:-   *Due out Summer 2000*

___ copies of God Speaks on Work

@ £7.95 / US$12.95 / NZ$22.50   _____

Post and packing per book
US $3.50
Canada $7.95   Add p & p   _____
UK   .   £1.50
Europe   £2.00
All other   £3.00
NZ   NZ$3   Total _____
Australia   NZ$10

I enclose a cheque/International money order   y / n

Please charge my card — please circle: Visa   MasterCard

| | | | | Expires | | |

Name and address & **telephone number** of cardholder

_____

_____

_____

_____

Name and address to send books to if different from above

_____

_____

_____

_____

Make cheques payable to and send orders to:
North America
Book Clearing House, 46 Purdy Street, Harrison, NY 10528
UK, Europe and rest of the world
éco-logic books, 10-12 Picton Street, Bristol, BS6 5QA, UK
NZ, Australia
Felicia House, 94 Opawa Road, Christchurch 8002, NZ

God Speaks Collection

Please notify me of publication of future books in the **God Speaks** collection

Name _____

Address _____

_____

_____

Post/zip code _____

Country _____

Email _____

Send this form to:

Soulfodder Press, Speke House, Long Beach Road, Longwell Green, Bristol, BS15 6UA, U.K.

Or email: info@soulfodder.com

Privacy Statement
Your name will not be disclosed to third parties for any mailings, nor used for any purpose other than to keep you informed about future works in the **God Speaks** collection.

Notes